CLOTH & MEMORY {2}

EDITED BY LESLEY MILLAR

CREDITS

Published By	Salts Estates Ltd.
Editor	Lesley Millar
Editorial Assistant	Beverly Ayling-Smith
Line Editor	June Hill
Designer	Gerry Diebel
Design Assistant	Lily Diebel
Design and Production	www.directdesign.co.uk
Print	www.foxprintservices.co.uk
Japanese Translator	Mary Murata

CLOTH & MEMORY TEAM: Lesley Millar (Curator), June Hill (Co-ordinator), Jennifer Hallam (Advisor), Keiko Kawashima (Co-ordinator Japan)

ISBN 978-0-9516950-7-4

First printed in 2013. Copyright © 2013 Salts Estates Ltd.

Copyright © 2013 Lesley Millar
All rights reserved. The author has the right to be identified and credited as the originator of this copy as part of the Copyright, Designs and Patents Act 1988.

All credits for photographs of artists work are with the images.

Addition images have been supplied by Beverly Ayling-Smith and the Cloth & Memory team. Image page 12, Maurice van der Velden, iStock and image page 16, Warwick Lister-Kaye Photography, iStock.

The book Cloth & Memory {2} has been published in August 2013 in support of the exhibition 'Cloth & Memory {2}' curated by Lesley Millar, opening at Salts Mill in August 2013.

All rights reserved. The rights of all artists, writers and photographers to be identified as the author of their work has been asserted by them in accordance with sections 77 and 78 of the Copyright, Designs and Patents Act 1988.

No part of this publication may be reproduced, stored in a retrieval system or transmitted in any form or by any means, electronic, mechanical, photocopying, recording or otherwise, without the written permission of the copyright owners and publishers.

CONTENTS

A Salts Mill Perspective Zöe Silver	5
Salts Mill past & present Beverly Ayling-Smith and June Hill	8
A UCA Perspective Dr. Simon Ofield-Kerr	10
Cloth & Memory: fragments, re-constructions and re-creations Lesley Millar	11
Artists' CVs	112
Acknowledgements	118
Sponsors	119

THE ARTISTS

Machiko Agano - Japan	18
Jeanette Appleton – UK	22
Masae Bamba – Japan	26
Caroline Bartlett - UK	30
Hilary Bower - UK	34
Maxine Bristow – UK	38
Reece Clements - UK	42
Yasuko Fujino - Japan	46
Caren Garfen - UK	50
Rachel Gray - UK	54
Annie Harrison - UK	58
Diana Harrison - UK	62
Katharina Hinsberg - Germany	66
Peta Jacobs - UK	70
Philippa Lawrence - UK	74
Hannah Leighton-Boyce - UK	78
Yoriko Murayama - Japan	82
Celia Pym - UK	86
Kari Steihaug - Norway	90
Koji Takaki – Japan	94
Katsura Takasuka - Japan	98
Karina Thompson - UK	102
Yoriko Yoneyama – Japan	106

A SALTS MILL PERSPECTIVE

My father called himself a Romantic Capitalist. In the mid eighties, many saw shut-down Salts as a sandstone mausoleum for a shafted industry, but he saw possibilities of romance, and of capital. As soon as he got the keys in 1987, he created a giant art gallery filled with Hockneys on the ground floor. Again, opinion was divided: hard to imagine now, in the nation of Tate Modern, housed in old Bankside power station, and where pretty much every regeneration project comes with its own art space as standard.

One of the things of which Dad was, and we are, most proud, is that this building is a place of work for over 1000 people, many of them concentrating on the cutting edge of technology at companies like Radio Design and Pace. Art and life should be cheek by jowl, because - as Cloth & Memory {2} demonstrates - the materials that surround us become part of us, and we them, in the most macro and micro of ways.

Everyone at Salts is very proud to open up the room at the top of the Mill for this breathtaking show. The talent, commitment and energy of Professor Lesley Millar, June Hill and Jen Hallam, and of all the artists you see here today, is something to celebrate. Thank you to all of them, and thank *you* for coming.

ZOË SILVER

4000

EMPLOYMENT: AT ITS PEAK, SALTS MILL EMPLOYED 4,000 PEOPLE USING THE MOST MODERN TECHNOLOGY OF THE DAY. IN 2013, OVER 1000 PEOPLE WORK AT SALTS, SOME AT THE CUTTING EDGE OF SOME NEW TECHNOLOGIES...

225m

INVESTMENT: IN 1853, WHEN SALTS MILL WAS COMPLETED, IT WAS THE LARGEST FACTORY IN THE WORLD AND COST £100,000 TO BUILD. THAT'S THE EQUIVALENT OF £225MILLION IN TODAY'S MONEY...

SALTS STATS

IN ITS HEYDAY, SALTS MILL MANUFACTURED OVER 30

16,380

5600

PRODUCTION: IF SALTS MILL MANUFACTURED OVER 30,000 YARDS OR 18 MILES OF ALPACA CLOTH PER DAY... THAT'S NEARLY 5,600 MILES PER YEAR (ENOUGH TO REACH ALL THE WAY BACK TO PERU AS THE CROW FLIES).

THE SPINNING ROOM: THE ROOM AT THE TOP MEASURES 168 M LONG, AND CONTAINED 16,380 CAP SPINDLES FOR SPINNING YARN. RAW FLEECE ARRIVED AT THE TOP OF THE BUILDING AND WAS PROCESSED DOWN THROUGH THE BUILDING TO EMERGE AS FINISHED CLOTH...

'Let us go back in thought to 1853, and see the machinery of "the works" ready for starting. How different the aspect which meets the eye from that which was visible [at its opening] on that 20th September, when Mr. Salt gathered his numerous friends around him to keep high festival! Everything now has the appearance of business. The combing-shed, where the sumptuous banquet had been spread, is now filled with machinery of the most recent invention; the weaving-shed is covered with its acres of looms, where many hands stand ready for work; the warehouses are stored with wools, soon to pass through the necessary processes prior to becoming fabric. At last, the great steam-engines begin to move, sending their motive power into every part of the vast system, which, as if touched by a mysterious hand, wakes up into life; the complicated wheels begin to revolve, the ponderous frames to quiver, the spindles to whirl, and the shuttles to glide. Now, the silence of the place is broken by the din of machinery, in which the human voice is quite inaudible, and then comes forth the product of it all, the beautiful texture known as alpaca...'

(Sir Titus Salt: His Life and Its Lessons, Rev. R. Balgarnie, 1877 P.92-3)

0 YARDS OR 18 MILES OF ALPACA CLOTH EVERY DAY...

'Between 1987 and 1997, the year of his premature death, [Jonathan Silver] created the world's biggest single collection of David Hockney images alongside high-tec industries, a Diner, art galleries, offices, a bookshop and a performance space. He converted a run-down textile mill at the bottom of a hill in a village three miles outside Bradford into a place now visited by thousands annually. I watched him do this and wrote the book 'Salt & Silver: A Story of Hope', a double biography of Titus Salt, the industrialist who built the mill in 1853, and Silver, the former men's wear shop owner, who restored and revived the building's magnificence. Silver, who loathed bureaucracy, never had a blueprint or masterplan. He started off with 53 David Hockney pictures which he put round the walls of a former spinning shed of 10,000 square feet. Admission to see them was, and remains, free. Like the farmer in the movie 'Field of Dreams', who builds a baseball pitch in the middle of one of his cornfields, Silver had a dream. His consisted of combining culture and commerce and making the result exciting and profitable.'

(Jim Greenhalf, Blogspot Friday 1 June 2012. http://jimgreenhalf.blogspot.co.uk)

A UCA PERSPECTIVE

This exhibition is important to the University for the Creative Arts because it represents so many of our past strengths and future ambitions. At UCA we are committed to maintaining the long history of bringing together extraordinary creativity with carefully acquired craft skills, which has characterized the British art school tradition for over 150 years. At our campus in Farnham, you will still find workshops dedicated to glass, ceramics and constructed textiles, sitting alongside and indeed integrating the latest digital technologies. Amongst the spinning and weaving of the textile workshop, the chemistry of the dye room and the challenges of the design studio, our students acquire and develop the knowledge and skills of previous generations, producing 'cloth' that stretches and challenges expectations.

The work in this exhibition is sited in the conceptual and physical space, where industry, the college and the domestic intertwine. It is important that in this meeting, time and space is found for the most conceptual and critical of reflections and productions. Lesley Millar's curatorial work has so effectively demonstrated the resonance that craft makers, artists and designers from across the world – who work in, around and through these designations – are finding through the literal fabrication of material criticality and conceptual creativity. It is vital that universities like UCA maintain, in these most challenging times, a commitment to material forms of research that are challenging and indeed beautiful.

Last year UCA created a new School of Crafts & Design, against the prevailing trend in HE, which incorporates the internationally recognized Craft Study Centre. This exhibition represents the values of the new School and our commitment to the past and future of investigating and materially stretching the definitions of cloth.

DR. SIMON OFIELD-KERR
VICE-CHANCELLOR
UNIVERSITY FOR THE CREATIVE ARTS

WHAT IS CLOTH TO ME?

"An auntie of a friend of mine, a very old lady, had never been to school, just locked up in a harem. One day I bought her a spindle. I bought her that because I am very interested in magic and I was sure the old lady would be able to tell us a lot about this and she did. She told us many things to do with the magic of spinning, which was fascinating and she was so happy that I had bought her the spindle. She said: 'I will make you a blanket'. The next time I came she had spun the wool and she had woven it and it was a very thin white blanket and for me it carries a powerful history."

"When I was just seven years old, there was a small party at home. My mother told me to wear rather ordinary clothes for a home party, but I begged her to allow me to wear the dress that my grandmother had bought me for my birthday one year earlier. I worked hard to help my mother, however when I was bringing sliced watermelons to the guests, I fell down. Splashes of red juice of the watermelon dyed my favourite dress. My grandmother was at the party. It made me so sad that my dress was stained and also I felt so sorry to my grandmother. About one week later, my grandmother came to my house and gave me a gift of otedama (beanbags) that Japanese children play with, which she had made using unstained part of my dress and a number of pieces of cloth of her different kimono. This is a wonderful memory for me."

"One of my pleasantest times was when I was choosing materials for where I live. It was for some cushions and the only really good pair of curtains I have ever had and I can remember spending about three days just going through the rails in all the swanky shops in Fulham and smelling the silk and a whole book of just different shades of rose, plum silk of various textures. It was terrific."[1]

1 - Unless otherwise stated, memories of cloth are taken from the video 'What Is Cloth To Me?' Becker and Millar (2005)

MEMORY

'...memories are blended, not laid down independently once and for all, and are reconstructed rather than reproduced.'[2]

We take history to be a linear construct: day follows day, year follows year. We live from one present moment to the next present moment, from experience to experience. We use our memories to tell our story, to connect to the stories of others, to bear witness and to create myths. But, unlike learned memories for example a poem or a multiplication table, memories of experiences are not fixed or unchangeable, stored within some filing system in the mind, accessible at will. They are fugitive, often coming unbidden responding to an unlooked for prompt, pieced together and re-constructed from the fragmented images released from the folds of the memory. Dissolving, slipping through the porous membrane of time, conflating experiences: memories are the wayward threads we use to reconstruct the narrative of our life.

Memory is a re-creative act, each time we remember we re-construct, rather than re-live, the experience: 'The remembered past and the moment of recall overlap without being identical.'[3] Remembering becomes a memory of the last remembering, re-visited by the self that exists in the present: shaded, changed, layered and stitched together. Memories are not passive, they come and they go, with shifting levels of importance, sometimes ambiguous and sometimes with piercing sharpness: 'mental constructions, created in the present moment, according to the demands of the present.'[4]

Memory is not only re-constructive, it is also destructive, it eliminates, wipes out: 'memory mangles and transforms its materials, tending to obliterate as well as construct.'[5] Such eradication leads to transformation in the re-construction of the memory, even leading to 'a past which was never present.'[6] In the Japanese film 'After Life'[7] the newly dead are helped to sift through their memories to find the one defining moment in their life. In order to remember this moment, they have to recognize it. Slowly they strip back the layers of remembering until they reach the essential feeling of the moment. They then work with the helpers to re-create that memory on film with all the ephemeral props associated with film artifice, what Hilary Mantel terms a 'Proustian cine-film'[8]. Once this is achieved, the dead person is then released to re-live that moment for eternity. The re-construction of that memory and re-creation of that moment demonstrates both the blending of memory and that "we don't choose between experiences, we choose between memories of experiences."[9]

2 - Sutton, John (1998). *Philosophy and Memory Traces*. Cambridge. Cambridge University Press. P.2
3 - Ricoeur, Paul & Changeux, Jean-Pierre. (2000). 'What Makes Us Think' (tr. DeBevoise) in *Memory* (2008) Byatt, A.S & Harvey Wood, Harriet (Eds). London. Vintage. P.184
4 - Fernyhough, Charles (2012). *Pieces of Light*. London. Profile Books. P.6
5 - Sutton, John. P.18
6 - *ibid* P.73
7 - Kore-Eda, Hirokazu (Director). (2007). *After Life*. Japan. Viewed 1st June 2013
8 - Mantel, Hilary (2003) *Giving up the ghost*. London. Fourth Estate. P.24
9 - Kahneman Daniel. *The riddle of experience vs. memory*, Best Brain Supplements (TED)

WHAT IS CLOTH TO ME?

"White curtains at an open window, gently moving in the breeze."

"Being wrapped in bath towels after coming out of the sea."

"Blue and white checked tablecloth on the kitchen table."

"Starched napkins folded in the shape of an upturned cone on the restaurant table."

"The secret/shaming/revealing red stain on my dress."

"The sound of the cloth being pulled and rolled out on the counter of the fabric shop."

"The scratchy feel on my arms and neck from my new organza party frock."

"The softness of the cashmere jumper worn by my partner."

"The sharp brilliance of the colours of the saris in the early morning light of Mysore."

"The sound of sheets on the clothes-line, flapping in the wind."

"Sleeping on the newly laundered sheets which still smell of the fresh air."[10]

Unless otherwise stated, memories of cloth are taken from the video 'What Is Cloth To Me?' Becker and Millar (2005)

10 - Author's own memories

MEMORY, CLOTH AND **THE BODY**

'Movements of the body, the only movements there are, mark this membrane. Again and again the approach to touch its surface, to press, to rub, to mark. What are inscribed are the signs of passing.'[11]

We experience the world through our senses; our skin is the active medium through which we process information. Remembering is also a physical act, taking place in the brain, in the neural networks of the body, and on the skin itself, forming memories that are both visual and sensory. Memory is not only a result of experience but also of feeling: '...hormones produced outside the brain, notably adrenaline and its neurotransmitter relative noradrenaline, are engaged in determining what is remembered....In this sense learning and remembering - memory - is a property not of individual synapses or nerve cells or brains, but of an entire organism, the person.'[12]

Our body holds our history, familiar triggers will take us down familiar networks to the 'sediment of a particular past in a specific brain and body'.[13] When language - words - can no longer be recalled, the body still remembers. Descartes likened this to the passage of a needle through fabric, leaving a hole which closes up, but not entirely so that the next time the needle repeats the action the passage will be easier through the hole already made, rather than making a new one. Cloth and Memory.

Membrane, fold, thread and pattern: cloth and memory. The relationship between cloth and memory is a rich seam and one that has been discussed and developed by writers, curators and textile artists over the years. Yet the role played by cloth as the silent witness to our passing through life remains evocative and seductive. The haptic relationship between our bodies and the textiles which accompany us provides an alternative language of memory, one that can be used by the artist to locate memory in an object, a material thing. In this way memory is re-created in a re-visitable manner, but it is a transformed memory, providing indirect access to the past, what John Sutton describes as 'representation without resemblance.'[14] And which the artist Robert Morris has expressed as pointing to: 'the texture of that involvement, to that density of feeling, to the simultaneous recovery and loss that memory delivers to us, that particular kind of death we never escape.'[15]

Fragmentation, marking/staining, re-construction, disintegration: cloth, memory and the body. We layer, piece and embroider the fragments to make a whole, but the stains have already 'disrupted the continuity',[16] edges are not bound, the threads fall away and are gathered up to be blended and spun into another re-constructed fragment. The textile designer Reiko Sudo said 'I am interested in the life of fibres and textiles, how they are reborn and recycled.'[17] As with cloth, so with memory.

11 - Morris, Robert in conversation with W.J.T Mitchell (1994) Artforum vol 32, no. 8. pp86-92 reprinted in *Memory*. (2012) Farr, I. (Ed.) pub. London and Cambridge MA Whitechapel Art Gallery and MIT Press. PP.92-3
12 - Rose, Steven. 'Memories are made of this' in *Memory* (2008) Byatt, A.S & Harvey Wood, Harriet (Eds). P.64
13 - Sutton, John (1998). *Philosophy and Memory Traces*. Cambridge. Cambridge University Press. P.18
14 - *ibid* P.58
15 - Morris, Robert. P.92
16 - Sorkin, Jenni (2001). 'Stain: On Cloth, Stigma and Shame' in *Third Text 14*, no. 53 P.77
17 - Millar, Lesley (2005). Interview with Reiko Sudo in *2121: the textile vision of Reiko Sudo and NUNO*. Epsom. University College for the Creative Arts. P.18

WHAT IS CLOTH TO ME?

"Tribal textiles contain memories of other times. In Afghanistan there are textiles containing the pattern of the sea. In Afghanistan you don't find the sea but some of the textile patterns are evocative of the sea."

'…moments I remembered, I might have again and pass on to you,… through this weaving.' [18]

'The smell of the weave studio: of a lustrous worsted yarn, dyed a deep, resonant tumeric yellow and taut on the loom, waiting for the interweaving of the warm, glowing chestnut dyed weft that I am wrapping around the shuttle.' [19]

"The sound of a taut piece of cloth stretched on an embroidery frame when a linen thread is being pulled through."

"My aunt makes every child who is born in the family its own blanket. She sews strips together and then cuts them, shifts them along one, re-sews it, cuts it and shifts it along one. It takes a while but she has a good eight or nine months when she can make these blankets and she gives them to everyone. It is funny because everyone still has theirs, as a grown up you have it and you have the memory of my aunt making these and she still does, for the new generation."

'At Salts Mill everything is larger. It is possible to feel the cloth of the past, not like a weight, but more like breath; the breath of the past, which in turn becomes my breath, and my version of cloth, which is redolent of my history, transformed by paint into a metaphor of a memory of cloth. The grandeur, the generosity of Salts encourages the memory to avoid the narrow focus of given moments, more to experience that unravelling of cloth and how it appears against a broader backdrop.' [20]

Unless otherwise stated, memories of cloth are taken from the video
'What Is Cloth To Me?' Becker and Millar (2005)

18 - Tuttle Richard. (2004) *Indonesian Textiles* ed Kahlenberg Mary Hunt. Chicago. Art Media Resources. P20
19 - Millar, Lesley. (2008) Paper delivered at the Design Centre London 6.10.2008
20 - White, Bob (2012). *Cloth and Memory*. Tunbridge Wells. Direct Design Books. P12

CLOTH, MEMORY AND SALTS MILL

Cloth: its making and use, its relationship to the body, all combine to provide the artist with a near perfect medium for the development of ideas concerning memory. Cloth retains the marks of wear and use, an ever present remembrance of what was. Cloth and memory share so many words and allusions: threads, folds, stains, piecing, patching, layering...When the opportunity was presented to relate this theme to a particular building created for making cloth, the symbiosis and the challenge were irresistible. Salts Mill was built to house the workers and the machinery necessary for the delivery, sorting, carding, spinning, washing, dyeing, weaving, finishing and sending out of cloth. Such potent associations are rendered even more evocative when placed in the context of a room in which the traces of cloth, the making of cloth are seeping through the floors and the walls.

When Salts Mill was opened in 1853 it was the most modern mill in the world, the first to offer all aspects of the production of cloth in one building. Now the 168m Spinning Room is empty but, within the absence, the memories of the production are still present. A room that was once full of the overwhelming noise from the machines now seems to hold a weight of silence as powerful as the previous tumult of sound. The history of Salts Mill and the past importance of textiles in the surrounding area is everywhere, coupled with the remaining evidence of Titus Salt's vision to provide a working and living environment where people could lead healthy and virtuous lives. The placing of highly contemporary, site-sensitive textile art at Salts Mill represents a significant drawing together of past and present practice, and so the re-construction of memory begins, embodied in the creation of works of art that take cloth as their starting point.

Each of the artists in Cloth & Memory {2} has responded to this place, this vast empty/not-empty space. Some with direct references to the history of Salts Mill or the history of the making of textiles; others have taken a more personal approach, placing private memories within the space. The works range from large scale interventions in space to highly intimate insertions within the fabric of the building. Peta Jacobs, Reece Clements, Caren Garfen, Annie Harrison, Jeanette Appleton, Caroline Bartlett, Rachel Gray, Hannah Leighton-Boyce, Philippa Lawrence and Hilary Bower all directly reference the lives and experiences of people who worked at Salts Mill and lived in Saltaire. Diana Harrison, Karina Thompson, Katharina Hinsberg, Yoriko Murayama and Maxine Bristow have created work in response to the building itself. Yasuko Fujino's work is remarkable in its bringing together memory and cloth across the centuries and continents. Celia Pym, Machiko Agano, Yoriko Yoneyama, Masae Bamba and Kari Steihaug each bring personal and performative elements to the theme. Koji Takaki de-constructs and re-constructs elements relating to other times and places, and Katsura Takasuka stands alone in his re-construction of the weight of life passed.

Together these works offer the opportunity for reflection on the nature of memory, its fragmentation and re-construction, its transformation and re-creation, and the symbiotic relationship between cloth and memory. The works are a physical re-construction of a moment (or moments) before the moment of looking, the viewing of the past transcribed through the present. Is this a memory? Or the memory of a memory?

The main technique of Yuzen dyeing uses a paste as a resist dye on the fabric and the removal of the paste after dyeing reveals the colour and pattern. This is called 'Yuzen Nagashi'. When all the paste has gone, the complete design appeared with brilliant colour in the water; this is a most emotional moment in the whole process of Yuzen dye.

I remember that they used to wash Yuzen dyed kimono fabric in Kamo river in Kyoto when I was a little child. We could see the long silk fabrics through the water, and artisans were shaking the fabrics in the water to take off the paste.

That kind of a daily scene was common about 50 years ago, not only in Kyoto but also everywhere they could get pure water in rivers all around Japan, such as Kanazawa, Tokamachi and Tokyo. Yuzen fabric used to exist closely with running river water in my memory in Japan. This has now disappeared because we need to keep the river water clean.

MACHIKO AGANO {JAPAN}

We Japanese used to think that water is not so valuable, for we used to be surrounded by large quantity of water everywhere in Japan. We used to say "spend money like water" meaning non-value. We couldn't imagine to buy water in old days. I now realize that we didn't pay attention to keep our environment clean or pure at that time. Yuzen Nagashi is just an example but we had similar circumstances elsewhere for many decades. We have to rethink how to relate with natural resources once more.

I decided to make inkjet printed fabrics using the photo images of old Yuzen kimono fabrics and make the shapes long and narrow, like running river water. The mirror sheeting on the reverse of each piece combines the visitor's own reflection in the mirror with the fabric images. I am not using the old kimono fabrics directly in my work, because it's just from my old memory not the actual fabric.

I would like the visitors to see my work as a fabric running river. And then, I would like them to know that we used to have such culture which coexisted with nature in old days but now are facing some difficulties in Japan. We have to avoid environmental pollution and to continue to keep our culture for future.

TITLE: THE RIVER
INSTALLATION
MATERIALS: inkjet printed polyester mirror sheet

"I was brought up in Kobe and I remember when I was a child the owners of the kimono shop would bring the fabrics to our home and they would show the fabrics and my mother would select which ones she would like made up into kimono for herself, for me and for my elder sister." {MACHIKO AGANO}

CURATOR'S NOTES: "I have had the privilege of working with Machiko Agano on several projects and she never fails to surprise me. This time she has created a work with both deeply personal resonances and ones that are important on a global scale. The weaving and dyeing of kimono fabric were central to Japanese culture and textile production for millennia, both in the studio and in the factory. 50 years ago, when she was a child, kimono sales were 100 times what they are today. She describes how, as she was growing up, all women wore kimono: her mother, grandmother, aunt, cousins...and how important it is that she herself wears kimono at special occasions, to keep the link with the past and because she now works with textiles. In her current work she is using that place which kimono holds in Japanese culture to bring to our attention the global price we pay for what we want. The work is beautiful, contemporary and shocking in its underlying theme." {LESLEY MILLAR}

MACHIKO AGANO {JAPAN}

Felt is a silencing material. It absorbs sound and memory.

The continual line of miniature cloth lengths hold motionless memories in their folds, of the expansive noise and moving threads of the spinning machines, within the intimate quiet recesses of the bobbin holders.

Not all detail is revealed, colour and surfaces hide within, as with the original Salts sample books of which only two remain. Specific cultural colours of social history and patterns influenced by colonialism only emerge when unfolding the pages. An enticing suggestion of the secrets glimpsed within are the frayed threads slipping between the paper edges.

JEANETTE APPLETON {UK}

The exposed tangled edge of threads are in contrast to the worn cloth fragments carrying traces of human activities and lives embedded within. A shadow which we have to seek, a peer into the folds for the individual.

Marks of hand labour: labelling and classifying, collected and stacked from the ledgers and pattern books from later local mills. Lines of materials ordered and cloth made, the product of dexterity, skills and inventiveness.

Constructing the miniatures evoke childhood reminiscences as thread is unravelled from bobbins saved from a visit to a silk mill where a great uncle worked. Or a mother's collection of wooden spools of thread; an inherited line of collections and creativity.

The line of mass production is represented by the use of industrial made needle felt created by the artist during a residency at Huddersfield University, retaining memories of previous projects and working spaces. It is manipulated into folding book forms by hand felting additional fibres and threads, including alpaca, silk and cotton.

The labelled books suggest a souvenir, an object which moves history into one's personal space. A commodified memory of a heritage site and a cultural experience. Picking up threads of past lives.

TITLE: PRODUCTION LINE : PEOPLES' LIVES
INSTALLATION: recesses 31 x 93 x 28 cm with individual works of various sizes from 15 x 5 x 12 to 21 x 10 x 20 cm
MATERIALS: Artist made needle felt, merino wool tops, various fibres and threads including alpaca and silk. Second hand scarves and fabric. Transfer prints and stiffening medium

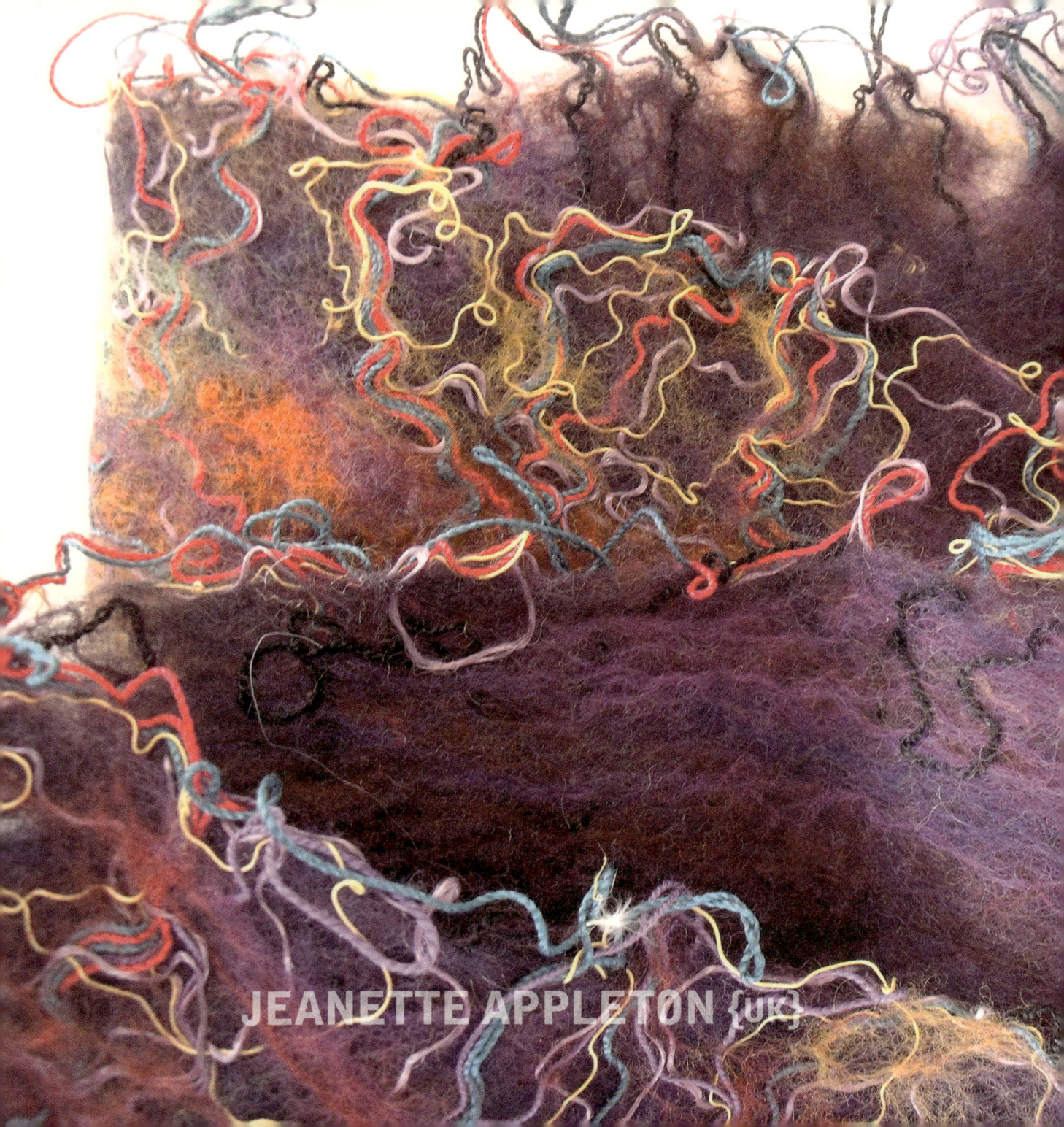

 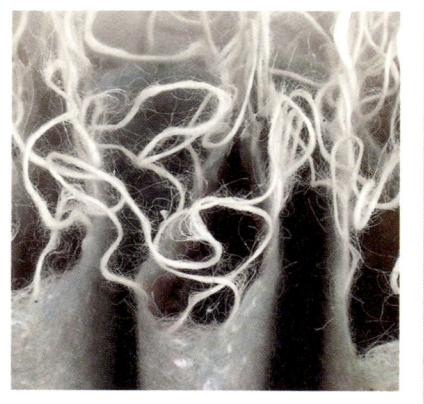 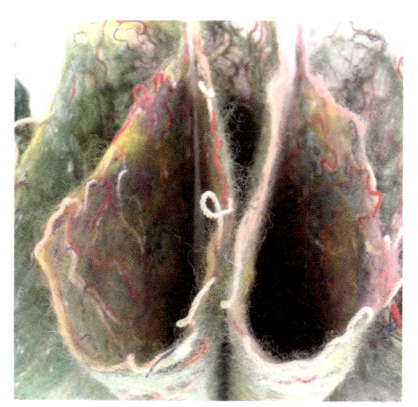

CURATOR'S NOTES: "The discrepancy between the size of the Spinning Room and that of Jeanette Appleton's work speaks volumes about the thousands of lives that have passed unmarked through the room. And volume is the key word: volume in terms of machine noise; volume in terms of books/ledgers. The noise that once dominated the room, and the silence which now fills the space finds its equivalence in Appleton's material of choice: felt - the industrial use of which is to dampen sound. The day ledger and the original pattern book, with the frayed edges of the cloths spilling beyond the pages; books that are the record of the skill and inventiveness of the workers in the mill. These are the starting points for the felt books placed within the walls of the Spinning Room. The felt holding the silent memories and actual traces of the past - copies of ledger entries, patterns from the pattern book, threads from Appleton's own collection from her mother and from her great uncle who was a silk weaver in Suffolk."
{LESLEY MILLAR}

"One specific memory which links with my current practice: my bare foot alighting from under my patchwork quilt, onto a pegged wool rug. It was made from unravelled woollen jumpers, so the crimp had a special feel between the toes. The image was of a lamb prancing in a meadow full of wild flowers. Drawn and pegged on sacking, my mother's childhood memories greeted me every morning. This detail of nature gave me a very early way of looking and continues in my soul. It was her escape into longing and nostalgia, from everyday practicalities. Watching her embroider delicate and perfect stitches into transfer printed crinoline ladies in front of thatched cottages and English herbaceous borders. This nostalgia of place and memory is a focus in my current practice, but towards tourism and ecological concerns." {JEANETTE APPLETON}

I used my daughter's 'nonsense' characters and I screen printed them on 10 different kinds of cloth - cotton, linen, mixtures, all natural fibres. I printed with nori, then I dyed the cloth with indigo. The text remains white. The text is printed over the whole cloth and then cut into different size strips. I only want to show the edge so I decided to layer the strips of cloth. I sandwiched many layers of the cloths between wooden slats and then dipped the cloths into the indigo dye so that it would give a natural stain on the cloth. It is a kind of shibori.

In this work I wanted to put the memory of my daughter into cloth because I am a textile artist. Cloth is very familiar to people. Through my work I hope people will have their own memories. When people see this work they only recognize cloth but I want people to feel water by looking at the work. When I was pregnant I felt water at all times. I felt as if I and the world are floating in water. I was researching and discovered the story of Helen Keller, who understood water only through touch and so I thought about knowing through seeing, hearing and touch.

MASAE BAMBA {JAPAN}

TITLE: FLOATING LETTERS, FALLING WORDS
INSTALLATION: 350 × 250 cm
MATERIALS: cotton cloth, linen cloth

"My grandmother was a professional kimono maker.

One day, she made a mistake on a customer's precious furisode kimono. This event left a deep impression on my young mind; 'Cut fabric can never be put back together again'." {MASAE BAMBA}

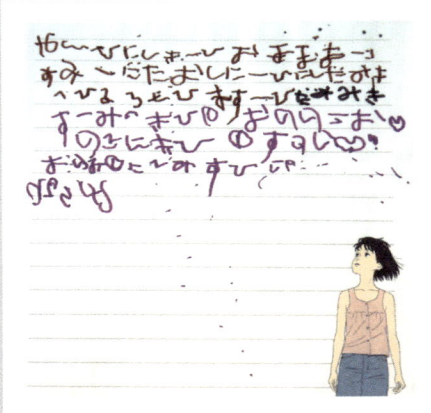

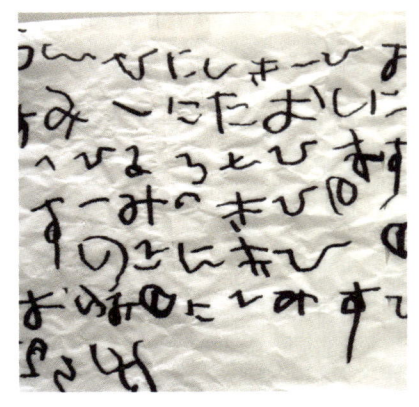

CURATOR'S NOTES: "Masae Bamba's indigo sea of cloth and symbols has resonance on so many levels: personal, cultural, global and material. The overt narrative concerns the first written text by her daughter, meant to say 'I love you Mummy' but in fact has no meaning, just approximately copied random Japanese characters. Bamba recognised this as a pivotal moment, the moment when communication between mother and daughter shifts away from the intuitive and haptic towards the use of a mediated form of communication. This memory is combined with two other.

The first the connection Bamba felt with water when she was pregnant with her daughter: her relationship with water as a primordial and connecting fluid. The second, a Japanese story as to how the dictionary was made: the letters were floating on the sea and people took their fishing nets and caught them and laid them out to form words. The cloth is soaked with indigo dye, but the non-words remain, floating along the edges, like the spume of a wave, unreadable but with an eloquence beyond spoken and written language." {LESLEY MILLAR}

MASAE BAMBA {JAPAN}

My original thoughts had been to make big work for such a big space but my responses to the site itself made me think about the intimacies of lives lived out here in a day-to-day routine of repetitious activity, of the human interactions and intimacies amongst the clatter of machinery. The walls themselves seemed to seep cloth and I imagine wool, pushing through the built outer skin of the building leaking into it with the smells and oils of its production. Whilst the materiality of production is absent, residues still remain inserted into cracks and clinging to metal beams. There is a sense of loss, of growth and decay, ruptures, cracks and regeneration, residues and traces. I think of skin, bone, membrane; a layered dermis and of webs of social, industrial, public and private relations, processes and materiality connecting the building itself with the idea of cloth as silent witness to the intimacies and routines of our daily lives. Touch, rhythm, repetitious movement. The haptic.

CAROLINE BARTLETT {UK}

The spinning hall is now silenced and emptied, stilled from being a place of noise, activity and industrial scale production where lives were lived out in repetitious production. There is a strong sense of presence, and absence, of a bygone era of industrial manufacture in which industries such as textiles and ceramics were so central.

The embroidery hoops are stretched with woollen cloth and into each is set a small porcelain roundel imprinted with an impression taken from a fragment of textiles; folded, creased, crumpled, stitched, manufactured. Spreading out from the ossified porcelain impression, and continuing the imagery, a web of stitching appears and disappears just under the skin of the cloth within the hoop. These glimpsed 'drawings' range from the more descriptive in interpretation to the more abstract but the clues can be found in the porcelain impression. The fabric will in some instances adopt markings and a depth of colour as though soaking up a history of spillages, stains and oils from the floor.

TITLE: STILLED
INSTALLATION: 7.5 x 1.58 x 2 metres
MATERIALS: porcelain, embroidery hoops, cotton thread, miscellaneous fabrics, stitched and dyed woollen cloth

"Clearing the house after my mother died I found her old rag bag. Up to the age of 11, she had made all my clothes and in the scrap bag were the carefully rolled and bound remnants of these dressmaking activities, each bundle taking me straight back to this part of my childhood in Africa and an item she had so carefully constructed; an instant mnemonic to a time and place through a glimpse of chocolate brown dress with stripes of turquoise animals, a red corduroy dressing gown… These bundles had migrated with us back to the UK and moved house with us on several occasions." {CAROLINE BARTLETT}

CURATOR'S NOTES: "Caroline Bartlett is exploring the hidden and the held. What is held in the silence of a room which was once so deafeningly noisy; what is hidden in the folds of cloth and the folds of memory. What has disappeared through the ruptures and cracks of the building and what has been lost through material disintegration and the fragmentation of memories. What we see are traces and surfaces, hinting but never revealing. As with memory, the view is partial, the story incomplete, reconstructed from fragments, and finding its own order.

The silent dignity of these works, holding memories of memories, contain so many contradictions/tensions: between the weight of the porcelain and the stretched fabric, between the preciousness of embroidery and the abject nature of the stained, and apparently abandoned work, between the private and the public." {LESLEY MILLAR}

CAROLINE BARTLETT

What first struck me on entering the roof space at Salts Mill was the sheer scale and then the sense of past presences, both human and non-human. The sense of production; the human endeavour on many levels seeping out of the air and echoing around is still strong. Much of what remains appears to be left to wait, in silence and in a quiet stillness with no particular purpose now, but hints at a previous existence and experience and is intrinsic to its present tangible atmosphere.

The hanging 'sacks' rest on the floor, on top of collected debris and dust from around the mill. They act as a metaphor for the repetition of making, of human physicality, of a memory, of loss, of containment, of holding and of silence; of a space, not empty but filled. Collectively they create a presence, a body of being. The use of basic, natural and utilitarian materials is necessary and holds memories of crafting, of making and of a human touch. Each 'sack' is filled with substance to give weight: sawdust; other gathered detritus.

HILARY BOWER {UK}

TITLE: OF HUMAN SIGNAGE - A VIEW OF SHADOWS
INSTALLATION: 7 sacks, each 198 x 92cm
MATERIALS: linen, calico, cotton muslin, cotton organdie, plywood, cotton rope, metal washers, webbing, aluminium, lead, waxed whipping twine and acrylic paints

This artist is sponsored by the Harley Foundation
Dedicated to Jane Elizabeth Haworth and Reverend Jack Cawthorne

HILARY BOWER {UK}

CURATOR'S NOTES: "The work has an overwhelming sensation of mass, of weight and of waiting. The beautifully constructed, almost, but not quite, human-size sacks rest on gatherings of detritus - the feeling being that they have been waiting, tethered in the space, in that place for a long time. Clamped, held, retained long enough for the dust in the air and peelings from the walls to have been blown through the room and settled around their bases. The sacks have been filled with another kind of dust: sawdust, creating the weight from the accumulation of dust, weighted by an amassing of the weightless, substance from the invisible. The surfaces of waxed calico have been worked into in different ways, responding to the marks on the floor of the room. The sacks also have additions, marked, pierced, rubbed away, seeming to have a purpose, the meaning of which is lost in time, leaving just the trace of the hand." {LESLEY MILLAR}

"My mum made our clothes and I was always aware of the feel of the fabrics and the smell. I loved to see her open up the dining table and lay out the patterns and start to cut out. I can still hear and sense the sound of the scissors cutting through the paper and fabric and echoing on the table underneath. It seemed really special. I loved the sense of cloth against the skin, in both handling and wearing and was aware of this in the places and homes we visited." {HILARY BOWER}

HILARY BOWER {UK}

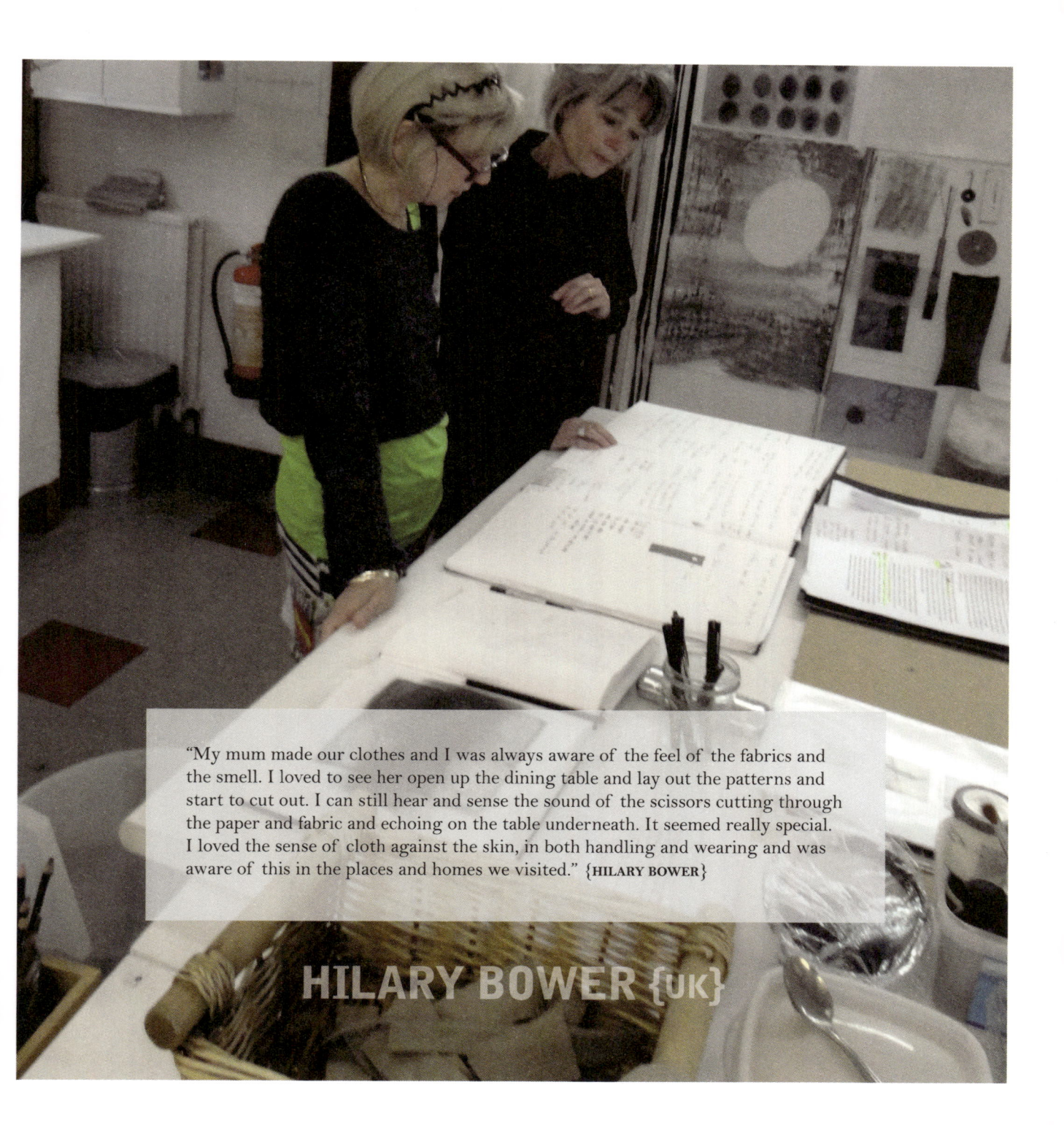

The Salts Mill exhibition provides an opportunity for reflection on models of subjectivity and the processes of attachment and detachment that are problematised through the intermediary agency of textile in relation to the framing (and reframing) of memory and heritage.

Key points of reference for the development of the work are tensions between stasis/mobility, proximity/distance, stability/instability that are potentially evoked through the experiential encounter. These paradoxical conditions are fundamental to the constitution of the precarious modern subject and particularly evident in the workings of heritage and memory. On the one hand memory and heritage (as a materialisation of collective memory) provide a sense of continuity and stability. As a way in which we make sense of ourselves in the present through reference to the past, they are important in the construction and representation of identity providing a sense of individual and social coherence in an ever-changing world. In its preservation and framing of the past, memory and heritage can evoke nostalgia for coherence and a unifying narrative of belonging. However, countering such constructs of seeming stability and continuity is the acknowledged mutability and contingency of heritage and memory. Both heritage and memory make 'selective use of the past for contemporary purposes'[1]; continually shaped by concerns and contexts of the present, they are fluid and dynamic, ever open to contestation and unable to provide us with stable meanings or unitary views of the past. As an alternative to the implied objective singular authority of 'official' history, memory is conceived as multiple, diverse, mutable, and contradictory. I would suggest that there are clear correlations here with the complex characteristics of cloth.

MAXINE BRISTOW {UK}

Thinking about the inherent contradictions that are evoked by the mutability of both cloth and memory, my intention for the exhibition is to establish a correspondence between more rigid structural frameworks and a series of curtains that provide a series of fluid fluctuating frames. Staged within these structural frameworks are smaller elements that ambiguously reference both the specific history of Salts Mill and the wider everyday functional and social conventions of textile through which we physically and psychologically connect with the world.

Offering a succession of fragmented tableaux, the aim is to maintain a productive tension between subjective attachment and detachment. On the one hand, the hope is to entice the viewer and evoke a heightened sensory awareness through the affective material sensuality and associative resonances of the work. Yet at the same time that the work facilitates a process of connectivity, the intention is to unsettle seeming stability through the staged artifice, semantic ambiguity, and fluctuating frameworks that physically and psychologically distance the viewer and resist subjective cohesion.

1. Ashworth and Graham, 2005, P.7, cited by Dowell, S, (2008) 'Heritage, Memory and Identity'. In: Graham, B.J. and Howard, P. *The Ashgate Research Companion to Heritage and Identity*. Aldershot, Burlington: Ashgate Publishing Limited. P.37.

MAXINE BRISTOW {UK}

TITLE: MUTABLE FRAME OF REFERENCE - INSTALLATION - MATERIALS: Timber, steel, woollen cloth, cotton cloth, faux leather, embroidery thread. SPONSOR: John White and Sons (Curriers) Ltd.

"Turquoise towelling, white broderie anglaise, blue gingham….spending hours making doll's house replicas from the remnants of our home sewn outfits."
{MAXINE BRISTOW}

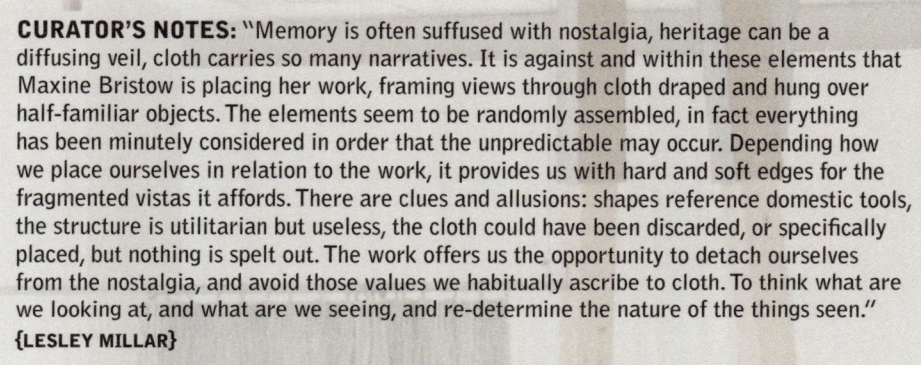

CURATOR'S NOTES: "Memory is often suffused with nostalgia, heritage can be a diffusing veil, cloth carries so many narratives. It is against and within these elements that Maxine Bristow is placing her work, framing views through cloth draped and hung over half-familiar objects. The elements seem to be randomly assembled, in fact everything has been minutely considered in order that the unpredictable may occur. Depending how we place ourselves in relation to the work, it provides us with hard and soft edges for the fragmented vistas it affords. There are clues and allusions: shapes reference domestic tools, the structure is utilitarian but useless, the cloth could have been discarded, or specifically placed, but nothing is spelt out. The work offers us the opportunity to detach ourselves from the nostalgia, and avoid those values we habitually ascribe to cloth. To think what are we looking at, and what are we seeing, and re-determine the nature of the things seen."
{LESLEY MILLAR}

MAXINE BRISTOW {UK}

I am a Bradford born artist. I would define my practice as mixed media textiles, often creating large scale textile installations. I create long lengths of handmade, often fragile felt that is then silk screen printed. These hand processes are then put to the mercy of modern laser technologies that are programmed with my digitally inputted drawings and mark making techniques. The juxtaposition of using both hand-made and modern machine technology is a commentary on how industry has changed, products that were once created by hand are now created by million pound machines.

My work takes hard objects and creates a visual metaphor in a more fragile and delicate medium that would break down if placed in the same setting as the original object. Themes I focus on include architecture, social history, the decline in British industry, the landscape, decay and natural patterns.

REECE CLEMENTS {UK}

"My grandma – Norma Wilson (nee Willoughby) – worked in the burling and mending department at Drummonds Mill. My great grandma – Mary Ellen Higgins (nee Willoughby) – worked in spinning in Salts for a short period. My great great grandma – Sarah Elizabeth Willoughby – worked at Salts in spinning. My great grandad – Jim Higgins – worked at Drummonds Mill in Bradford. My great grandma – Elizabeth Wilson – worked in the warping department of Masons Mill in Shipley. My great granddad – Gerald Wilson – was a boiler firer at Masons Mill. My mother – Susan Wilson – did some work experience while studying at Keighley College in the offices at Salts Mill." {REECE CLEMENTS}

REECE CLEMENTS (UK)

TITLE: THE FELT HAS ROOTS
INSTALLATION: 600 x 260 x 220cm - 280cm
MATERIALS: British wool tops, suit lengths, silk-screen printing and laser etchings
SPONSOR: Cardiff Metropolitan University - Textile Department

CURATOR'S NOTES: "Reece Clements and his work are deeply rooted in Salts Mill, Saltaire and Bradford. For several generations his family have worked at Salts Mill and lived in the area, therefore, although he is the youngest artist in the exhibition, more than any other, Reece Clements' life and memories are interwoven with those of Salts Mill. He is using felt, a material created by the locking of the fibres, trapping space, holding the memory of the hands that have created it. The screen printed and laser etched imagery form fragile layers based on the architecture of the mill and surrounding area and bring together traditional techniques and new technologies. The whole is resonant of time and the breakdown of materials as a result of time, of change, decay and rebirth in new ways and new forms." {LESLEY MILLAR}

(1) The click of the knitting machine cradle as it counts row after row was the sound of my childhood, each grandmother churning out different interpretations of jumpers and cardigans to dress their grandchildren in.

(2) One of my earliest memories from being a toddler is being inseparable from a Prince of Wales check flat cap; this subconscious connection to the stereotype of a Yorkshireman must only have been influenced by my granddad who always wore one to keep a chill from his head. {REECE CLEMENTS}

I found two episodes about memories: One is the episode about Anne Lister(1791-1840) who was born in Halifax. She is famous for her diary which she kept in code. Lister is often called "the first modern lesbian" for her clear self-knowledge. Her diaries contain more than 4,000,000 words and about a sixth of them—those concerning the intimate details of her romantic and sexual relationships—were written in code.

The other episode is about the traditional Nushu script. Nushu is a syllabic script, a simplification of Chinese characters that was used exclusively among women in the sex-segregated world in traditional southern China.

Memories are overlaid and remade many times, however faded. Nevertheless, women want to share the secret memories."Sharing" and "fading" seem to me contradiction. The theme of my new work is to visualize the existence of such memories which has such a contradiction. In order to express my theme, I chose the form of kimono as the container of the memories, because kimono is treated as a symbolic form of women in Japan. Into each kimono I weave coded memories.

YASUKO FUJINO {JAPAN}

The warp is very highly spun silk threads with the nori still in the yarn and each warp contains 3,600 threads over its 40cms width. For the Grand Weft I use a double shuttle with an S twist on one side and a Z twist on the other side. This keeps the cloth straight and flat. I work from the back. The supplementary weft is made up from many different yarns. I want to layer the images. In fact there are always 4 layers which overlap, but of course they change with each kimono.

These layers are a combination of print and weave which include a printed general motif that everyone can recognize, for example a bottle - this is the key to the 'code' of the work. There is also a printed colour on the overall white fabric which gives again a theme, for example green for garden, plus woven abstract supplementary wefts. I worry that the weave and the print will be perceived separately so I always cover the prints with a woven supplementary weft in order to integrate the images with the fabric. Doing this makes the edges not sharp, as the edges of memory are not sharp. For this I use either silver or gold thread. It takes a very long time, I can only weave 7 cm a day, but layering is very important for my work as each layer represents memory

TITLE: CLOUD Piece1: Fate - Piece2: Cipher - Piece3: Garden
INSTALLATION: 200 x 200 x 10cm
MATERIALS: silk, mohair, gold thread

YASUKO FUJINO {JAPAN}

"My grandmother's kimono was passed down to me from my mother. When I touched that kimono, I felt a strange sensation; I could feel the memories which were stored within the fabric." {YASUKO FUJINO}

CURATOR'S NOTES: "In the beautiful silk kimono woven by Yasuko Fujino she is bringing together East and West through the signs and symbols of coded language. The Nushu (Nu: women, Shu: language) secret language of the women from the Hunan province of southern China, and the self-invented code of Anne Lister in which she described her love affairs with women.

Fujino has chosen the kimono as a means of conveying her narrative of memory. Kimono, and the knowledge of how to weave kimono, are passed down through the generations. Kimono contain the memory of all woman's experience, the rules and rituals of being a woman. Fujino's kimono are woven with inlay and warp printing, layer upon layer, blending images, yarns, tensions and ideas.

The effect is cloth in which are embedded signs and symbols, many of which are familiar to us: butterflies, bicycles, bottles, and others which are much more ambiguous. Nothing is random but the meaning is not clear. Fujino calls the work 'Cipher' and as with the secret languages of Anne Lister and Hunan women the key to the code is necessary in order to access the content." {LESLEY MILLAR}

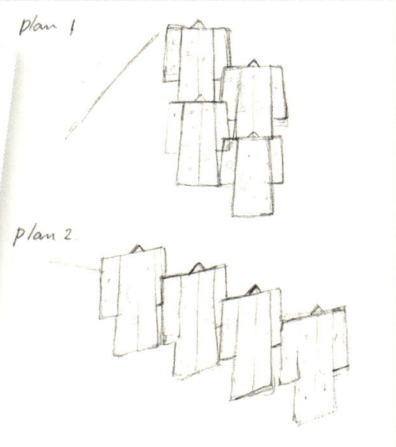

YASUKO FUJINO {JAPAN}

I have created an artwork in memory of, and in recognition of, the real women of Saltaire drawn from the 1891 census. Women who were born in the parish, and grew up, worked (in the textile industry), married and had children there.

I have researched a sample (1,000) of the population of Saltaire. All persons selected were born in the parish from 1826 onwards, and they have been subdivided into 6 sections:

- Female Mill Workers
- Male Mill Workers
- Female Other Occupations
- Male Other Occupations
- Wives
- Children/Scholars

In-depth study of the census has produced evidence that 160 single women were mill workers, and a further 42 had other occupations, e.g. dressmakers, milliners, etc. Fifty-one married women were entered of whom one-fifth were working. Of the latter, only three were employed in the mill, and none of these had children. Almost 390 children/scholars are accounted for.

CAREN GARFEN {UK}

A conclusion is thus drawn from the sample that, in almost all cases, once a female mill worker married, her life in the mill drew to a close and became centred on family and the home, leaving few occupations to combine with her new position as housewife.

REELS – Each reel will have its own 'memory plaque' with the woman's name, year of birth, age, marital status and occupation hand sewn onto a circular white ground which will be adhered to the face of the reel - the red ones signifying those who married, the blue ones referencing the plaques with the street names of Saltaire, most of which are named after the family of Titus Salt. Each plaque will have an 'S' symbol as an acknowledgement to both Titus Salt's and Jonathan Silver's vision.

APRON – The occupations of the women are hand sewn in pink onto one of the apron ties and on the second tie, the wide varieties of employment open to men taken from the 1891 census will be sewn in blue. Thus the apron will display one relatively short tie and one excessively long tie, illustrating the inequalities in occupational choices between males and females at that time.

TITLE: REEL LIVES, 1891
INSTALLATION
MATERIALS: hand embroidered cotton fabric, silk threads, vintage wooden spools, antique sewing tools, alpaca wool

REN GARFEN (UK)

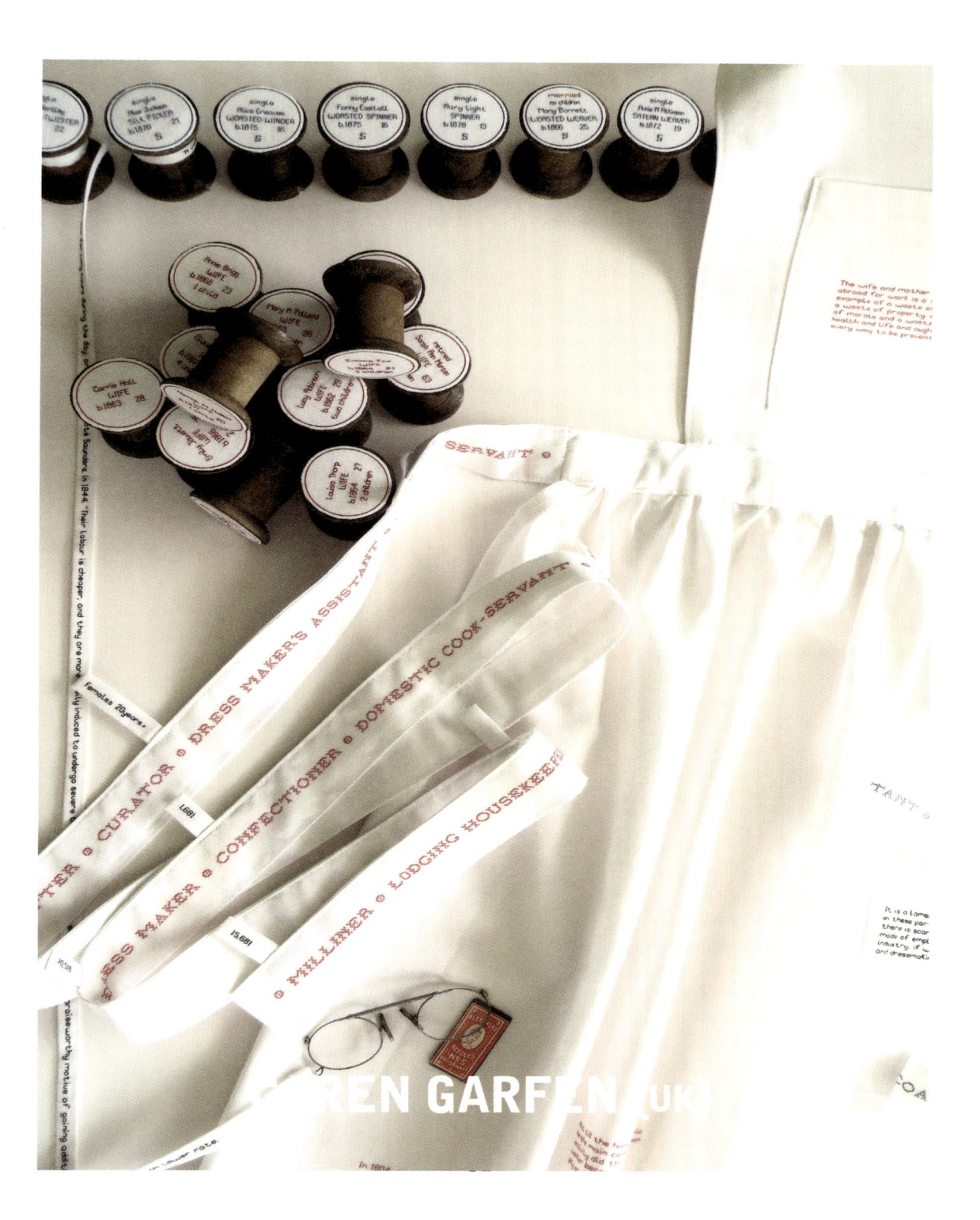

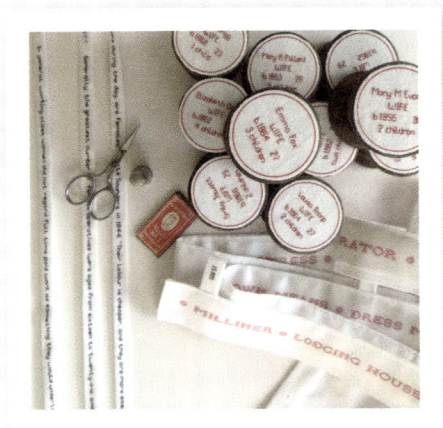

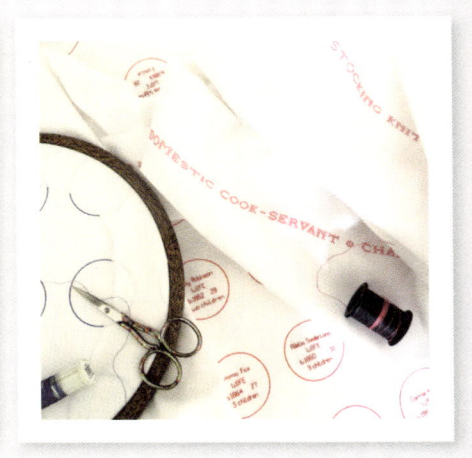

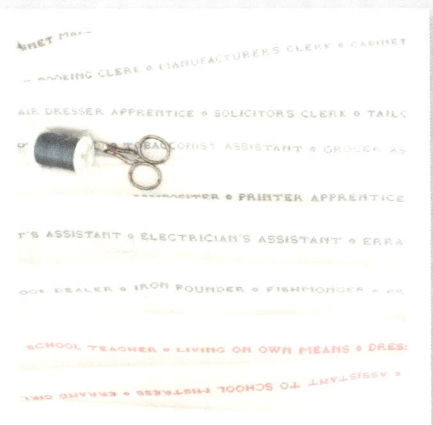

"I remember, as an eleven or twelve year old, being asked, as part of the school syllabus, to make a nightdress for our needlework class. We had to bring in some suitable material, and my mother said I could use a beautiful length of cream satin which she did not need. I made the bold decision that I would make a negligée which would match the shimmering, soft and luxurious silkiness. Every week I went to the lesson with an excuse of why I could not commence with the process. I would purposely forget the satin or the paper pattern, or I would tell the teacher that I could not decide which side to cut. At the end of the term, there was no negligée, and this wonderful material remained a complete whole. I felt very satisfied by this at the time…..I thought it was too special to use the scissors upon it, or perhaps I was simply afraid to cut into it!" {CAREN GARFEN}

CAREN GARFEN {UK}

CURATOR'S NOTES: "Caren Garfen's work for this exhibition is a remarkable translation of meticulous research into meticulous outcomes. She has assiduously tracked down and worked through ledgers documenting the facts concerning those who lived in Saltaire and were employed at Salts Mill at a certain time (1891). Her intention has been to make visible those lives which have disappeared. Working in the most painstaking hand-stitch, she re-presents this information in a manner that is direct, understandable and completely humane in her use of the tools and the domestic/work garment - the apron. The beautifully pristine work is a reflection on the pride taken in appearances and in a job well done which would have been prevalent at this time. Placing such white, starched and ironed work within the dust and decay of the former Spinning Room also parallels the battle it would have been in those time to achieve such unspoiled and spotless appearances." **{LESLEY MILLAR}**

I've always found the 'wrong' side - the inside of garments more interesting than the 'right' side. Turning a garment inside out reveals more: the structure, the method of construction, alterations, labels and wear and tear, darts and tucks, seams, padding and interfacing. The same is true of quilts: The Chapman Coverlet in the V&A collection dates from 1829 and is unfinished allowing the reverse to be seen, each piece of fabric still contains a paper template, supposedly the Chapmans' love letters but many appear to be domestic accounts.

The structure and method of making my patchworks is repetitious; going over and over, like memory, the patching, mending and layering is revisiting and also remaking, adding to and altering the story. Listening to Proust's 'In Search of Lost Time' while I stitch, layer, patch and mend confirms that tiny details are significant – that each time you look again and look closer there is more to see, that even everyday, simple and humble objects have stories to tell; in frayed and worn edges and unravelling stitches, marks and scratches or peeling paint there is evidence of life, industry and of time passing, there is drama in a single stitch.

RACHEL GRAY {UK}

TITLE: Shadow Pieces
INSTALLATION: 11 pieces each = 94 x 17cm
MATERIALS: Transfer printed and stitched silk, cotton gauze, silk organza and linen

RACHEL GRAY {UK}

"A collection of old dresses in the attic; a dark red velvet Edwardian dress, an evening dress of my grandmother's from the 1920's and my mother's 1950's white ball gown. I was fascinated by these historic fairy tale frocks and occasionally allowed to bring them down to unwrap and try on. I remember the weight of the dresses, the many layers of linings, underskirts and nets. The fabrics were aged and seemed almost ready to crumble. The large silk flowers tucked into the draped neckline of the evening dress were now faded, wilted and flat." {RACHEL GRAY}

CURATOR'S NOTES: "The fragmented layers of Rachel Gray's work represent a kind of material archive of vestigial traces. The work reveals and conceals the evidence of those lives which have touched and been touched by the cloth. In some cases the work looks as if it has emerged from the wall itself. I am particularly intrigued by those sections of the work in which she shows us the reverse side - the 'wrong' side, the side that exposes the traces of making, the private side, the side that touches the body. The references she is making to patching and mending are made all the more intense through the fragility of the material, the sense of the wear and the tear, rendering consequence to the fragments beyond their materiality." {LESLEY MILLAR}

RACHEL GRAY {UK}

Using visual arts techniques, I have been working to recover lost memories of place and to produce site-specific work that combines new technology and participatory practice as a means to explore elements of the past life of Salts Mill and Saltaire. This project is situated in my ongoing art practice, in which I uncover hidden narratives, and use the material qualities of site and story to create visual art which speaks of what Christian Boltanski calls 'small memories'. These small memories turn undifferentiated space into place, endowing it with value and giving people a sense of belonging. As de Certeau says 'Haunted places are the only ones people can live in.'

I have produced an audio visual and text piece which combine real-time recordings of mapmaking, with an audio commentary. Maps of Salts Mill have been drawn by people who have worked in, or lived alongside the Mill at different times in its past. Through the process of drawing, memories have surfaced about the place and the activities that took place there.

References: De Certeau 'Walking in the City', from *The Practice of Everyday Life*, Berkeley: University of California Press, 1984. Semin, D. Kuspit, D. Garb, T. Boltanski, C. Christian Boltanski, London, Phaidon 1997.

ANNIE HARRISON {UK}

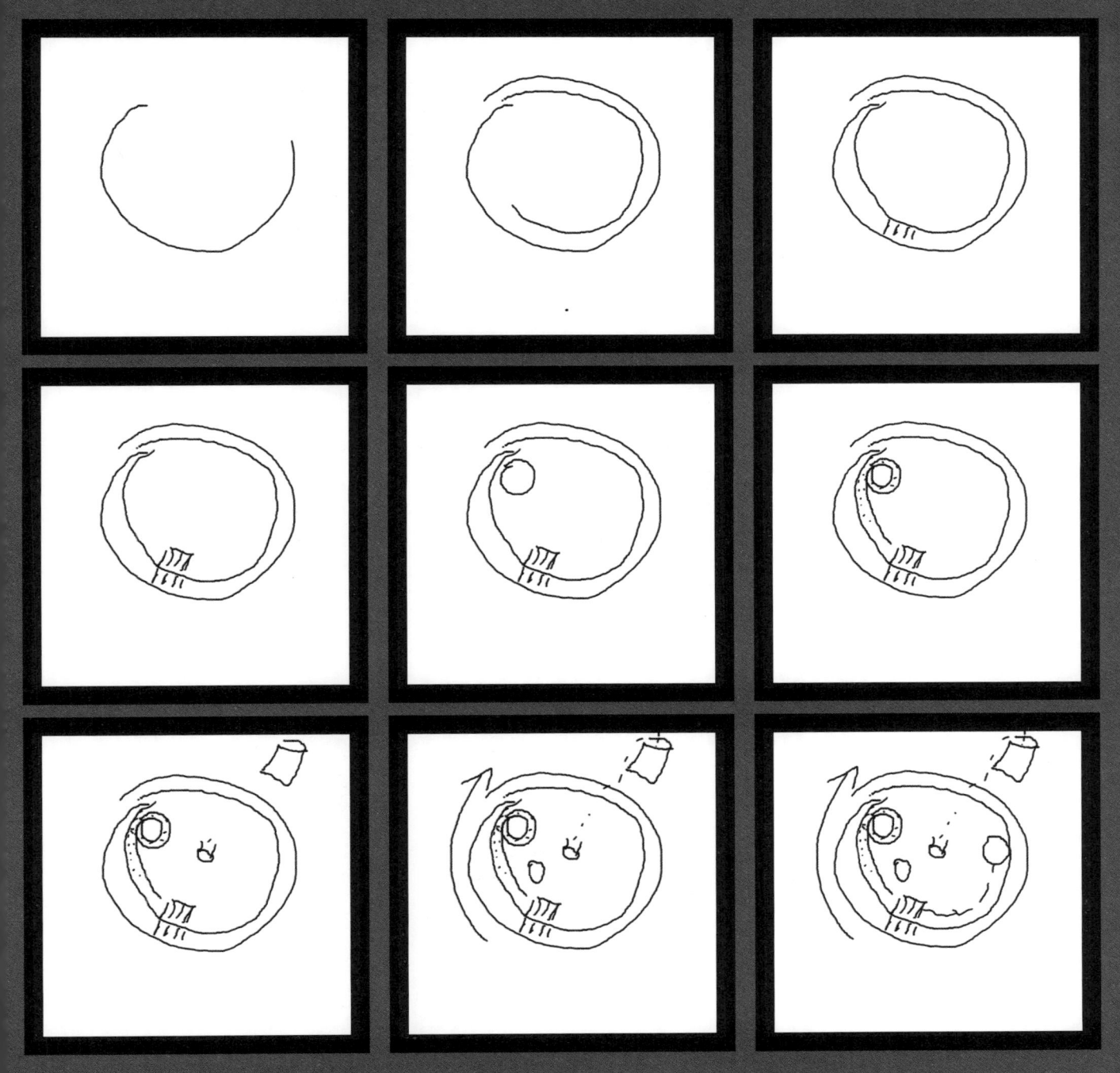

ANTONI JANOWICZ - COMBING MACHINE

CURATOR'S NOTES: "There is no cloth in Annie Harrison's work, yet the threads of cloth are everywhere present. In her videos there is the memory of cloth, or rather the memory of working with cloth, or more accurately the memory of working in or near the building in which the cloth was fabricated. These people talk and draw: their routes to work, their routes around the mill and as they draw they begin to re-imagine themselves taking that route, re-constructing the route and re-creating the experience. Annie Harrison's work takes the memories which survive in habits, embedded physical recollections and spontaneous reflexes and through drawing, she has used them to evoke other places and times." {LESLEY MILLAR}

Original images reproduced by kind permission of Shipley College, Saltaire Archive.

"I remember as a child, I had a candlewick bedspread – I can't remember the colour, it may have been a faded yellow. I used to love to chew the tufts of thread – they created a resistance between my teeth that was irresistible." {ANNIE HARRISON}

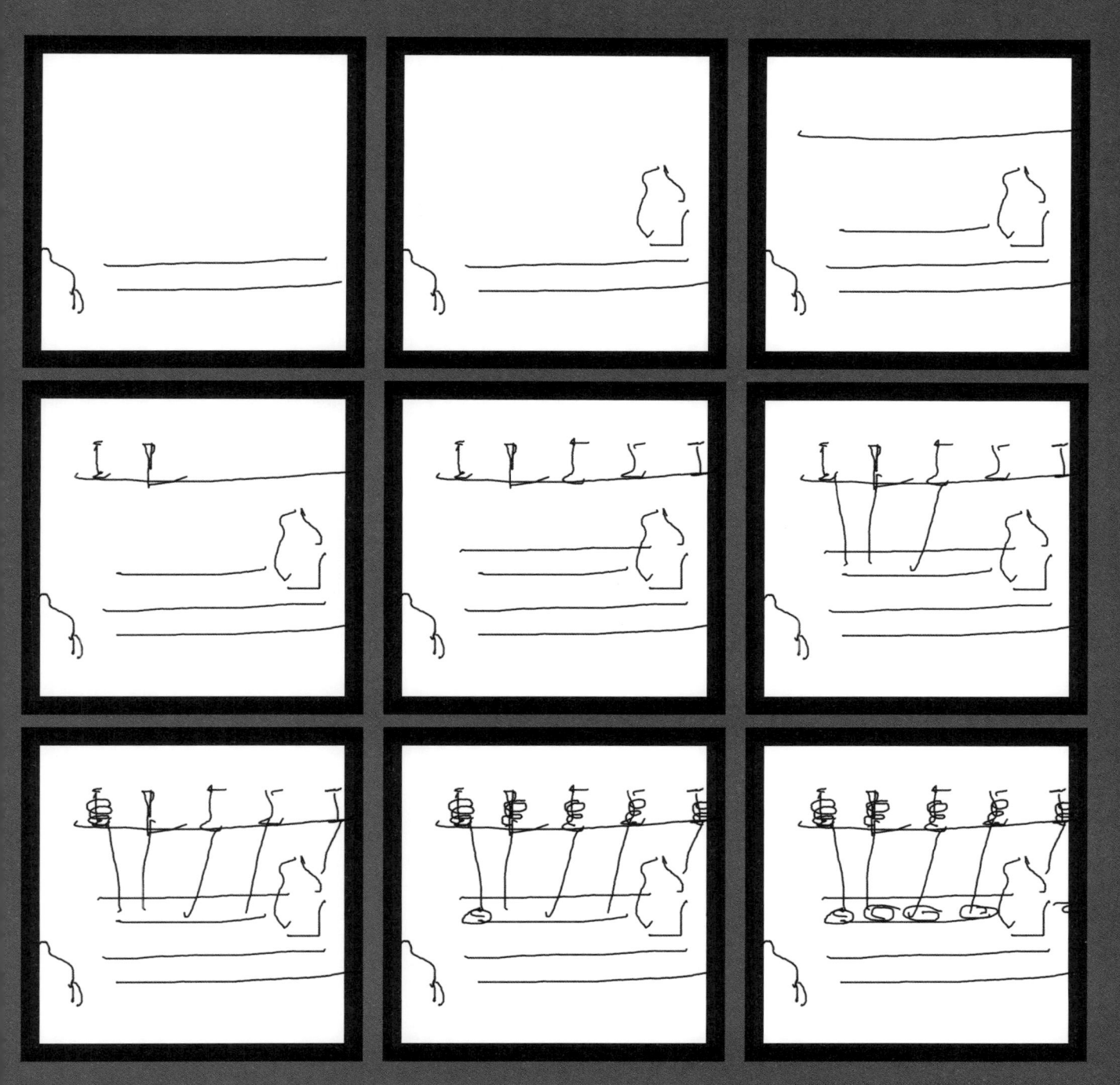

VAL WOOLLEY - VISITING THE WINDING ROOM

My response to the top floor of the disused spinning mill at Salts was firstly what a huge and beautiful empty architectural space, and then the imagination takes over, and history floods in: noise, smells, machines and above all people, their entire working lives, lived out in one place, Saltaire, with its philanthropic, support/living /work system.

Visually I was particularly interested in the floor, the large grey flagstones, irregular sized rectangles carefully fitted together to make this indestructible industrial surface. How these stones were fitted and the water stains from a leaking roof were inspiring, so it seemed appropriate to work towards something at ground level to be walked around observed from above.

DIANA HARRISON {UK}

Using recycled handkerchiefs (that had been in everyday use until paper took over), was the initial idea. I started collecting from friends, family, vintage and charity shops, market stalls and two were picked up off the street. They are all different but all cotton and square. Men's, women's, children's, each with its own past; used, washed, stained, worn or boxed, kept for special occasions, given as gifts, hand embroidered or monogrammed.

Once they were all dyed black they came together, lost their individuality apart from the different qualities and weights of cotton from very fine voile to plain sheeting cotton. Whilst printing and bleaching out the dye the details, weave, initials, embroidery and edges all came back to life; each handkerchief was worked as a separate unit.

Whilst stitching them together, by hand, with a loose fishbone stitch and in keeping with the quality of the original items, the size of each handkerchief dictated where they fitted in the whole, and the subsequent composition of the piece takes on a random growing quality that could be added to in the future.

TITLE: HANDKERCHIEFS
INSTALLATION: approx 4 x 2.5 metres
MATERIALS: recycled cotton handkerchiefs

DIANA HARRISON {uk}

CURATOR'S NOTES: "The work Diana Harrison has created for this exhibition is atypical. She is known internationally for her ground-breaking work using quilting techniques, yet for cloth and memory - a subject which seems tailor-made for a quilter - the only reference to quilts is a visual one in the patchwork layout of handkerchiefs. The ubiquitous paper hankie has rendered the cloth handkerchief as almost a memory, but back in the heydays of production at the mill, a 'proper' cloth handkerchief would have been a luxury item, only for use on Sundays and special days. The rest of the time it would have been a piece of rag or nothing. The second-hand handkerchiefs Diana Harrison has collected, dyed and sewn together were all once prized possessions, and through her attention they are now precious again. Laid out on the floor, as they are in the exhibition, they are like so many memorials to the unknown owner/worker." {LESLEY MILLAR}

"My memory goes back to early childhood remembering a well washed, soft corner of flannelette cot sheet with a particular blanket stitched edge. I have no visual memory of this cloth only the tactile, bedtime comfort it provided."
{DIANA HARRISON}

With my work, I link up at the point where, back then, the chain of textile production ended in the old spinning area: using spun thread. On site, I measured out the floor space of the room with a long red thread that comprises its length (L) and width (W). The thread took measure of the room even as it was measured according to it – and at the end it was cut off.

The thread remains uncut in its entire length when I set up the measured length and width as warp and weft on a weaving frame. The thread, bearing the measurement of the room, keeps this "in mind", so to speak. And it communicates and visualizes this memory when the line of thread becomes a (woven) surface again that stems from the dimensions of the room, in exact correspondence to it. In this manner, the actual floor measurements are translated into a model of the floor, in a scale of 1:100.

KATHARINA HINSBERG {GERMANY}

TITLE: WARP + WEFT
INSTALLATION: 1.556 x 0.161 metres
MATERIALS: Cotton thread, red, 161.7 metres

KATHARINA HINSBERG {GERMANY}

"In the car I sit on the back seat. Summer lies over the lake, and reeds are visible among the poplars. The car window has been shoved wide open to the front. Earlier, out on the decrepit veranda, my father had sewn the covers for the car seats from stiff tent canvas, and stretched it between the metal frames.

They talk. My mother's blouse is made of white cotton crêpe, embroidered in sumptuous red at the neck and shoulders, tied with a thin string in the front. She drives barefoot, her hair pinned up. What does "political" mean? Her big basket purse holds only the little kitchen knife with the coloured plastic handle. We wait in the car until she returns with gigantic bouquets of chamomile, campion, Queen Anne's lace, and willow herb, swaying in her arms in lavish abundance."
{KATHARINA HINSBERG}

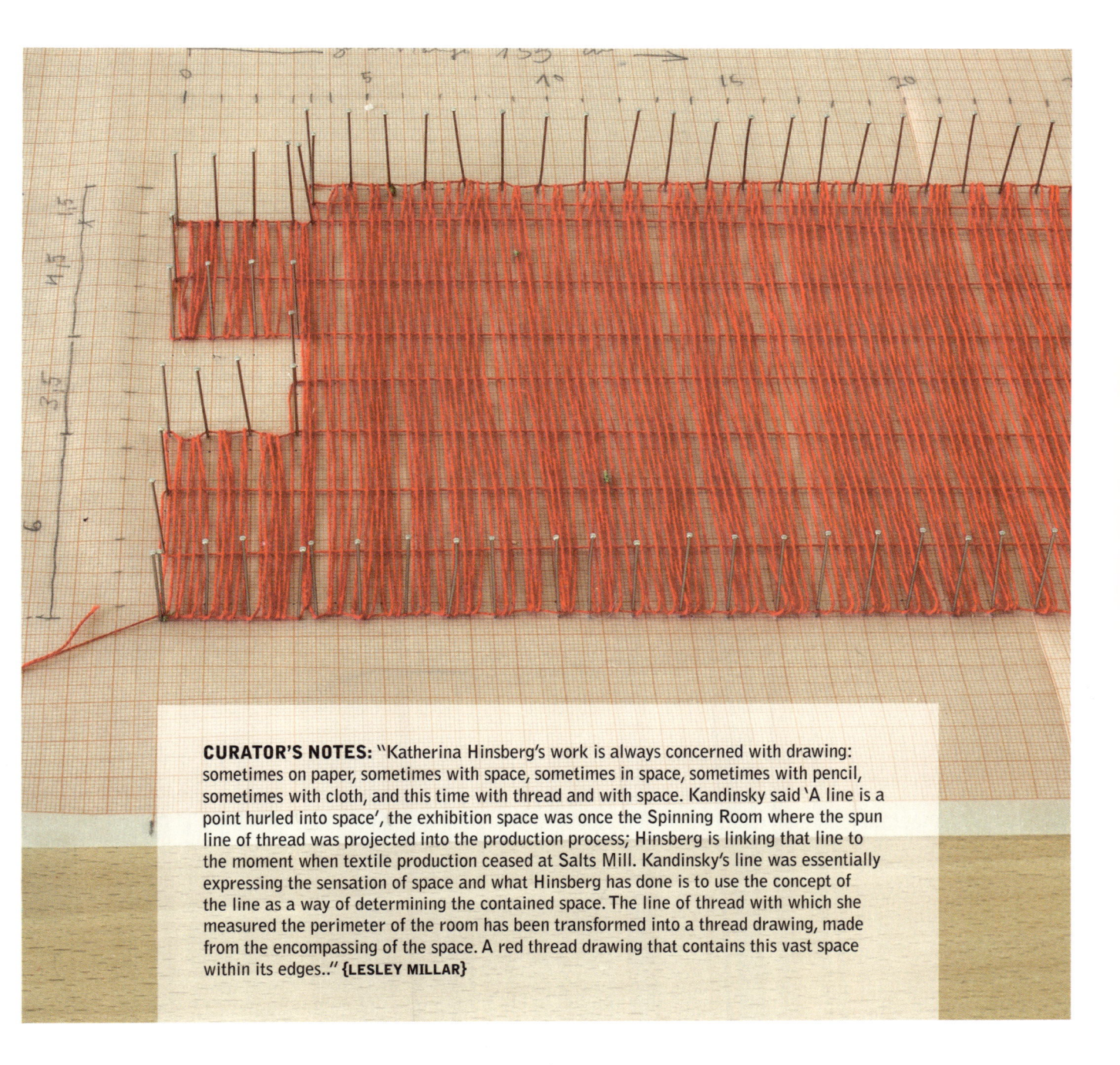

CURATOR'S NOTES: "Katherina Hinsberg's work is always concerned with drawing: sometimes on paper, sometimes with space, sometimes in space, sometimes with pencil, sometimes with cloth, and this time with thread and with space. Kandinsky said 'A line is a point hurled into space', the exhibition space was once the Spinning Room where the spun line of thread was projected into the production process; Hinsberg is linking that line to the moment when textile production ceased at Salts Mill. Kandinsky's line was essentially expressing the sensation of space and what Hinsberg has done is to use the concept of the line as a way of determining the contained space. The line of thread with which she measured the perimeter of the room has been transformed into a thread drawing, made from the encompassing of the space. A red thread drawing that contains this vast space within its edges.." {LESLEY MILLAR}

TITLE: SHADOWS OF DISTINCTION
INSTALLATION: 6 x 2.25 metres
MATERIALS: Cotton fabric, screen-printed cotton/silk fabric, Devoré

PETA JACOBS {UK}

In the darkened space of the 'foyer' to the Spinning Room hangs a wide swathe of cloth capturing shadows of life-size ghosts of men in elegant clothing from a time gone by. The shadows are as immaterial and ephemeral as memory itself. When you venture behind the installation, your own shadows merge with those of the men. On this side the material substance of the cloth is revealed. The fabric has been eroded by a devoré process that leaves delicate silk threads that tenuously hold the cloth together. The imprinted traces of the image are unravelling, fragmented and fading; the spaces between remain intact.

Otherworldly sounds fill the space. As you listen to the sounds they disappear and others take their places, an encounter with presence and absence, in and out of time. The recording captures the sound of Franki Brewer weaving on a hand loom, however, it has been altered by a time distortion – slowed down to reveal the spaces between the sounds.

The smells of the machine oil and lanolin that have infused into the very fabric of the building and are still perceptible in the space. Past and present co-exist and there is an intriguing juxtaposition of what has happened before and the present moment.

This piece commemorates the heyday of the textile industry when Bradford was the wool capital of the world. The image is taken from an iconic photograph of the prosperous men of distinction gathered at the Bradford Wool Exchange in the early 1950s. The sounds of weaving within this piece represent the burgeoning new shoots in the present-day woven textile industry. Franki Brewer is my daughter, a woven textile designer and co-owner of Dash and Miller. I was inspired by her creativity and love of textiles and followed in her footsteps to go back to university to study textiles myself.

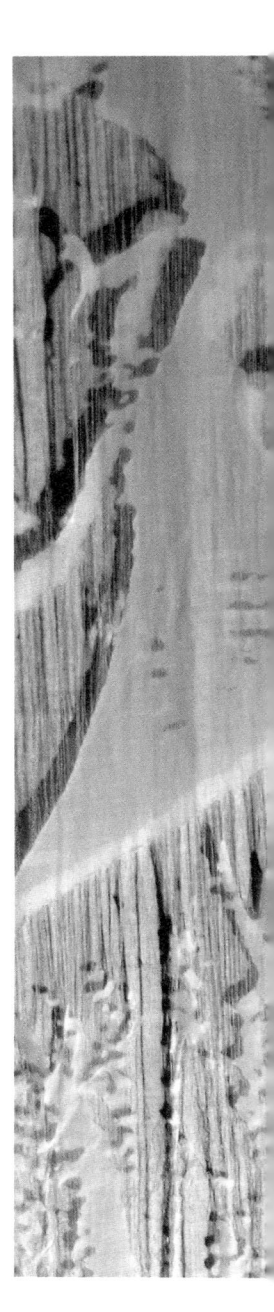

PETA JACOBS {UK}

CURATOR'S NOTES: "The starting point for Peta Jacobs' work is an archive photograph of the members of the Bradford Wool Exchange in 1953/54. These sombre men, and it is all men, look out from the photograph, solid, still secure in their place in society. Did they know how soon it would all change? Now they and the industry they represented have almost disappeared, only traces left. Peta Jacobs has printed this image at an almost life-size scale, using her extraordinary skill with the Devoré technique. Devoré burns and destroys the fibres of the cloth in order to create its pattern - in this case image - and so we are seeing what is no longer there. Shadow men, made visible only by their absence, given form by the creative expertise of a woman." {LESLEY MILLAR}

"I am lying on my bed, my sandals neatly tucked underneath. I fidget, frustrated at having to endure 'rest-time' after lunch. I want to be playing. Yet, I soon settle as I become absorbed watching the play of light and shadows cast by the bright African sunshine through the cotton printed curtains which are dancing on the breeze through the open window. A rippling line of bright, bright light undulates where the cloth almost, but not quite, meets the sill. I am engrossed by a continually shifting dance of light, shadow, translucency and density. I am captivated, soothed and entertained." {PETA JACOBS}

height 2.25m

cloth = 5.76 metres

Screens.
⑫

Images.
144 x 75cm.

fabric - 147cm

fixings?

75cm
144cm

PETA JACOBS {UK}

Reading 'Textile Voices: 'A Century of Mill Life', I was struck by these words: 'The mill owned your house, it controlled your working day, it decided your friends (and your partner), it determined your health, it organised your leisure time and in some cases told you what to think, where to worship and how to vote'.

A small child would run errands for the mill and once employed he or she might spend their entire life at the mill. The building held the bodies and thoughts of hundreds of people and, as a consequence, the jobs they undertook shaped these people and became part of them. A mill worker's life was intimately entwined with that of the mill.

This interconnection of life within the mill and the idea of the fabric of the building, the fabric of life and the fabric of this specialized society provided huge scope for my own thought and research. As an artist concerned with issues of site, place and land, I am interested in the potential for cloth and the language of textiles to connect people to place. Initial considerations were to extend the metaphor of the land as a fabric that bears the marks and memory of industry by looking at routes associated with the wool trade, including packhorse bridges, paths and inns.

The exhibition has enabled me to use language directly. The way communities use language tells us a lot about culture and place and bears testament to the collective memory we have of place, of work and of ourselves.

I studied the impact of the textile trade upon our language, researching processes and techniques that were once part of daily life and have now become consigned to memory. I made a list into a poetic roll call of words associated with the business of weaving and life in the mill. The presented work speaks of the art of making fabric and the fabric of living. It also stands as a memory of the activities and of the people who worked in this trade on this site.

PHILIPPA LAWRENCE {UK}

The cloth was fabricated at William Halstead, a local mill, with the 'poem' woven into its selvedge. This collaboration was core to the project, enabling me to learn and to involve myself in the trade. The selvedge is cut away when the cloth is made into a garment but for me this discarded edge is vitally important because it represents the work of those who were central to this industry and this place but who may now be forgotten.

TURNING • RISING • WAKING • FALLING • SLEEPING • LIVING • HOPING • DRAWING • DREAMING • TRYING • STARTING • WALKING • WATCHING • WEIGHING • PULLING • WARNING • BREAKING • THINKING • HEFTING • SCOURING • RIGGING • STRETCHING • BALANCING • CORDING • HOLDING • ROVING • SHAKING • JOINING • LOOMING • BLENDING • OILING • FORMING • LIFTING • LOVING • COMBING • STORING • BURLING • CLEARING • STRAINING • WARPING • COUNTING • CARDING • PRAYING • SORTING • STROKING • LEANING • PINNING • PIECING • MACHINING • CARRYING • HANDLING • CLEANING • GRADING • SIZING • LOADING • TUNING • BREATHING • NUMBERING • BALLING • PACKING • BENDING • TALKING • THREADING • CUTTING • TWISTING • CRYING • SPINNING • CALLING • REACHING • RUNNING • MAKING • TALKING • MOUTHING • MENDING • REELING • SPOOLING • SIGNING • SENDING • SWEEPING • DANCING • MINDING • SHEDDING • WINDING • WANTING • WAITING • WORKING • CRAWLING • PICKING • SIGHING • FLITCHING • SHOUTING • CRABBING • FIGHTING • LAUGHING • MILLING • WASHING • DRESSING • HEATING • SMOOTHING • FOLDING • STEAMING • WEFTING • NIPPING • RESTING • YAWNING • STANDING • SLIDING • MEASURING • HIDING • ACHING • STOPPING • SITTING • WEAVING • SAMPLING • AGEING • WRAPPING • EATING • GIVING • TAKING • ASKING • DYING • BEATING • COATING • GUARDING • STREAMING • GILLING • PLEATING • MOURNING • SINGING • WRIGHTING • KNEELING • COUGHING • GROUNDING • READING • SHARING • LEARNING • SINGEING • LOSING • GROWING • KEEPING • FEELING • PERCHING • CARING • PASSING • DRAFTING • CONDITIONING • TENTERING • POLISHING • FINISHING • CLOSING • REPEATING •

TITLE: THE FABRIC OF MAKING
SIZE: 48 x 67 cm
MATERIALS: Inkjet print on Somerset Enhanced Velvet Radiant White, 330 gsm

"I have this memory: of standing in the playground leaning against the new school building when I was about 8-9 years old, picking and pulling the tiny balls of pilled fluff from my red school jumper and then carefully placing these into the gaps in the cement around one of the bricks. I can quite clearly see myself intent upon this and remember the concentration and sense of connection the action gave me."
{PIP LAWRENCE}

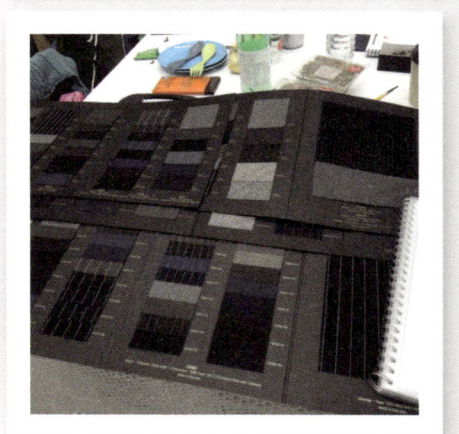

CURATOR'S NOTES: "Whatever Philippa Lawrence does, it is never what one expects. As an artist specialising in site-specific work, her relationship with place is the driving rationale, always developing and challenging her own methodology and responses. Most recently she has been working with the landscape, digging down and re-constructing, which in a way she has also been doing at Salts Mill. Digging down into history - researching all the words associated with the states and actions involved in the construction of cloth and weaving them into a relationship with words describing the states of living a life. Her decision to work with a local mill: William Halstead, reflects her immersion in the history of the place and the appropriateness of bringing together her ideas and industrial practice. Many hours and many discussions took place between Philippa Lawrence and Halstead's in the selection of the cloth and the positioning of the words along the selvedge. Much has been written about the intertwined history of cloth and language: text and textiles; with this piece Philippa Lawrence has embedded that history in a cloth that speaks of its own history and that of the people who have lived their lives in the making of the cloth." {LESLEY MILLAR}

PHILIPPA LAWRENCE {UK}

"Come and experience the never seen before views at Salts Mill"

When I first entered the Spinning Room, I was struck by the vast size of the space and emptiness. A space which would once have rung with the mechanical turn of progression was now empty: silence replacing the screeching and rattling of 120 spinning-machines, and calmness in an air once heavy with wool fibres, oil and heat. I was fascinated by this absence, and began looking for visible echoes and traces of the past.

In one of the alcoves recessed into the wall, I saw at the end of the small dark enclosure, a slotted cast iron grate and, as I focused on the small fissures of light shining through it, could see the rising tops of the workers' houses in Saltaire. I felt a gentle breeze, and heard voices and sounds travelling from other parts of the mill. I put my hand inside the empty space and found nestled within the damp crumbling stone and dust, a small piece of grey wool…

HANNAH LEIGHTON-BOYCE {UK}

My work explores experiences of time, and the creation of space; experiences and rhythms of time that go beyond the thresholds of language. I focus on specific 'moments of encounter' to explore how to make visible those experiences that sit on the realms of the felt and unseen, creating moments of suspension or pause through the play between ideas, materiality and process.

With the Victorian love of light 'trickery' and the first ever 'moving image' of Leeds Bridge being made in 1888, just 11 years after the final building at Salts Mill was completed, it felt fitting and appropriate to explore the animated 'moving' image created by the camera obscura in combination with the alcoves. The installation of 'The Windowless Shed Camera Obscura' invites viewers to experience these in almost a Victorian-like wonder, these 'never seen before' views from the fifth floor of the historic mill. The placing of cushions invite the visitor to sit and watch, contemplate the view and the building's history in hope of allowing time and space to slow and extend, creating a window both to the past and present.

TITLE: THE WINDOWLESS SHED CAMERA OBSCURA
INSTALLATION: installation in ventilation alcoves
MATERIALS: lens, wood, glass, (kneeling cushions - worsted cloth dyed with rust from Salts Mill, alpaca fibre)

HANNAH LEIGHTON-BOYCE {UK}

CURATOR'S NOTES: "In the vastness of the Spinning Room, Hannah's work is the most hidden, and could easily be overlooked. In this she is inviting us to think about the hidden experiences of those who worked there, experiences which are embedded in the fabric of the building. For the workers the tiny ventilation grills represented the only access to fresh air and their only fragmented, disconnected glimpse of the world outside. With the camera obscura Hannah is bringing the outside inside, but that view is not quite right, not real, upside down, unreachable. We have to translate what we are seeing and in so doing spend time realising that we can see the wind in the leaves, see the clouds shift by, see the view with fresh eyes. Fresh eyes that echo those of the Victorian workers in the mill who saw images created by a camera obscura for the first time. In order to see the work we are required to bodily engage with the building. We are required to kneel and peer into the dark ventilation grill Hannah has given us an entry point into the experiences and memories of those many who peopled the room before us." {LESLEY MILLAR}

"The curtains had been removed from their windows and were in the bin. I never really took much notice of them when they were hung in the windows, only perhaps to note that they were black, austere and were blocking the light, but at this moment I observed a flicker of wonder and connection.

Unlike the person who had decided they were no longer of use, I saw them not as worn out, threadbare curtains, no longer capable of doing their job but a surviving memory, a tangible piece of history embedded with time; I heard a story of someone's mother coming into the school to make blackout curtains during the war.

In light and shadow they remained. Due to their particular situation at a Quaker School, they hung in the windows of the East Wing for around seventy-three years as silent witness or 'conscientious objectors', hung in quiet protest to changes going on in the outside world.

The curtains speak of duration both in their marking and through the nature in which they were made by an extended process of analogue exposure; a palimpsest of light and the slow passing of time which opens up a space between the something felt and something seen." {HANNAH LEIGHTON-BOYCE}

HANNAH LEIGHTON-BOYCE {UK}

I feel there is a memory of the old textiles in the building, and therefore I have used the building as a symbol for memory. My plan was to weave the landscape of Saltaire using inkjet to print old and new photographs of Saltaire, printed onto Japanese paper. So that the image can still be understood when it is woven, I have enlarged it to four times its original size. The paper is then cut into fine strips and used as the wefts. This is a traditional Japanese method of weaving called Shifu. I have woven the brick patterns of Salts walls by traditional Kasuri warp Ikat technique. The images woven in this way are misty and indistinct, expressing memories, which are fading little by little. The shape of the cone is inspired by the cones for spinning the thread in the mill and each cone has different images.

YORIKO MURAYAMA {JAPAN}

TITLE: AND THEN
INSTALLATION: 6 elements, each 200 x 50 x 50cm
MATERIALS: sericin silk, abaca, Japanese paper

YORIKO MURAYAMA {JAPAN}

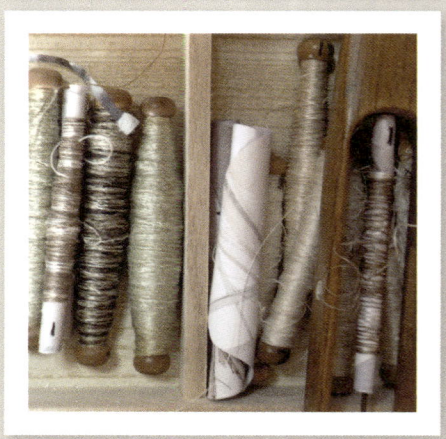

"When I was a child, my mother used to unpick old kimono and make them into futon quilts for the family. My own quilt had a dark pink background with a green pattern, made from a Meisen silk kimono from my grandmother's young days.

I loved that pattern so much that, at my request, my mother re-padded that quilt many times instead of making a new one from fresh fabric." {YORIKO MURAYAMA}

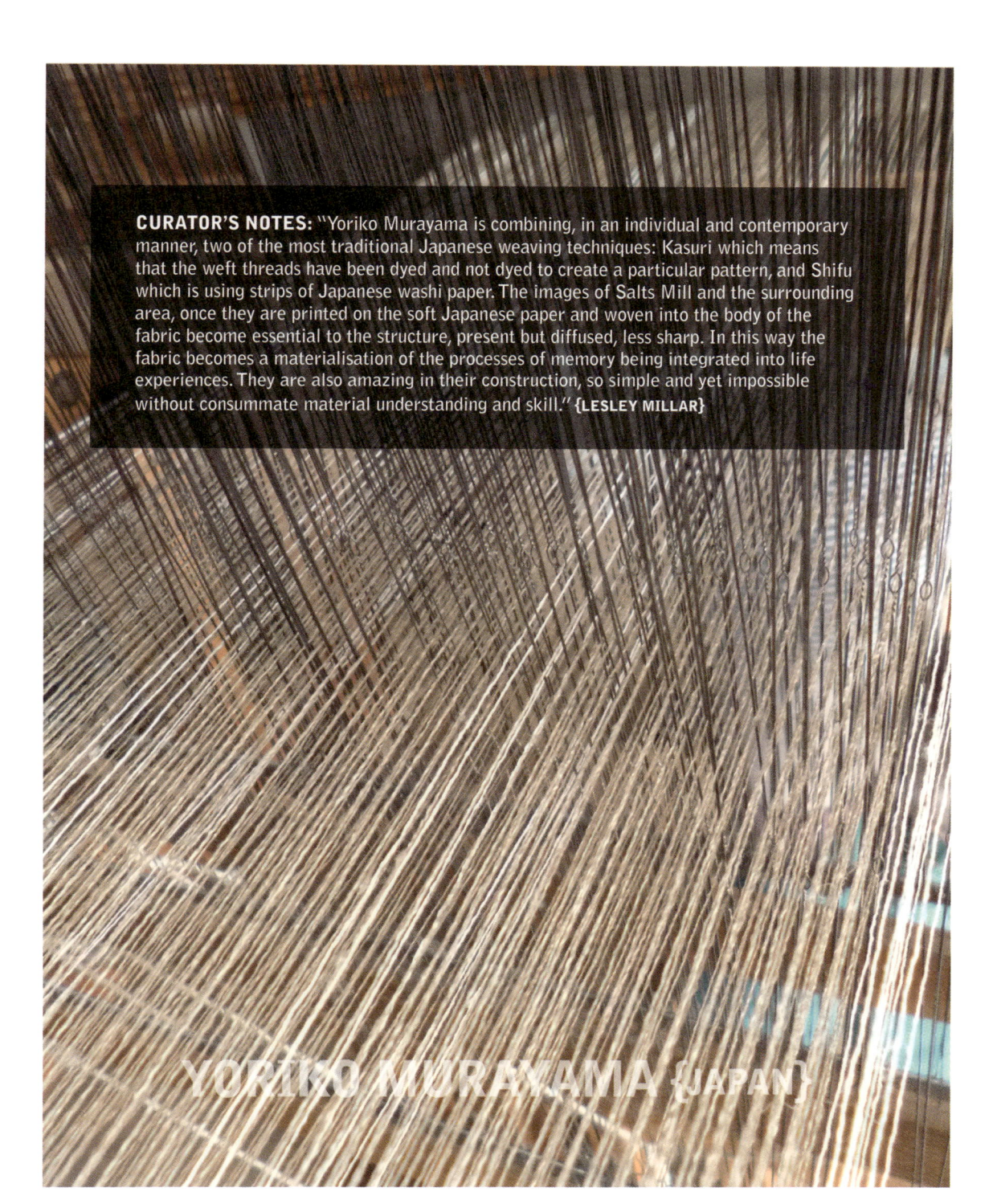

CURATOR'S NOTES: "Yoriko Murayama is combining, in an individual and contemporary manner, two of the most traditional Japanese weaving techniques: Kasuri which means that the weft threads have been dyed and not dyed to create a particular pattern, and Shifu which is using strips of Japanese washi paper. The images of Salts Mill and the surrounding area, once they are printed on the soft Japanese paper and woven into the body of the fabric become essential to the structure, present but diffused, less sharp. In this way the fabric becomes a materialisation of the processes of memory being integrated into life experiences. They are also amazing in their construction, so simple and yet impossible without consummate material understanding and skill." {LESLEY MILLAR}

YORIKO MURAYAMA {JAPAN}

CELIA PYM {UK}

On my first visit to the Spinning Room at Salts Mill, I felt like a detective. The absent activity of the spinners felt very strong. Deceptively empty there was lots of evidence of activity that used to happen in there. Layers of paint, shadows of where objects used to sit, old signage, coat hooks. It made me feel a bit like I recognized something, like a feeling of *déjà-vu* but could not put my finger on what I recognized.

I like to see how something is made, how it works. Darning is good at helping you understand an object, you darn it and you can figure out how it works, where it is strong and weak, how it was constructed, how it was used, loved – if you darn in an opposite colour to the colour of the original textile it highlights what has changed and that time has passed. Darning can be a tender activity. I had that in mind when I was preparing the new work for Cloth and Memory 2. And a process developed, I wanted to make something but alter it very gradually, so the change would happen with many small moves.

I knit a sweater and then cut it apart, re-knitting patches to fill the cut away holes and darning them in place, then darning together the cut away knitting. So that slowly the original sweater was replaced and then put back together again.

TITLE: BLUE DARNING
INSTALLATION: 120 x 70 x 20 cm (2 sweaters each approx. 60 x 70 x 20cm)
MATERIALS: wool and acrylic yarn

CELIA PYM {UK}

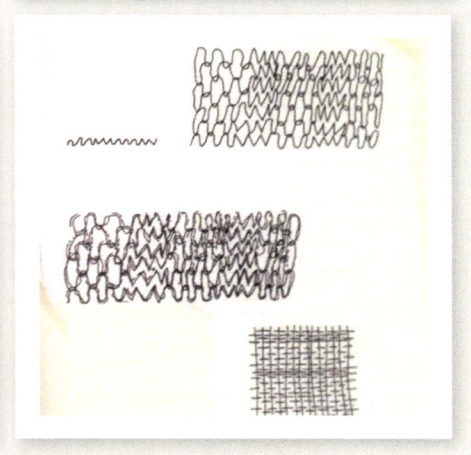

CURATOR'S NOTES: "The original title of this work was 'Stop Looking Like A Sweater' and alongside the drawings in her notebook was the phrase 'a thing but not a thing'. Both the room and the sweaters contain the memory of their original function but the Spinning Room at Salts no longer functions as a spinning room, and the sweaters don't function as sweaters. As memory is not fixed, but layered, so the constituent parts of the sweater have been layered and changed. How much difference and how much correspondence between the experience and the remembering, between the original sweater and the final piece, needs to exist for one to be the memory of the other? Knitting, cutting, patching and darning, re-constructing the sweaters - the second from the cut away fragments of the first; the first darned back together with patches from elsewhere. Eventually each is a memory, an echo of the original, as she says 'right, but not right'." {LESLEY MILLAR}

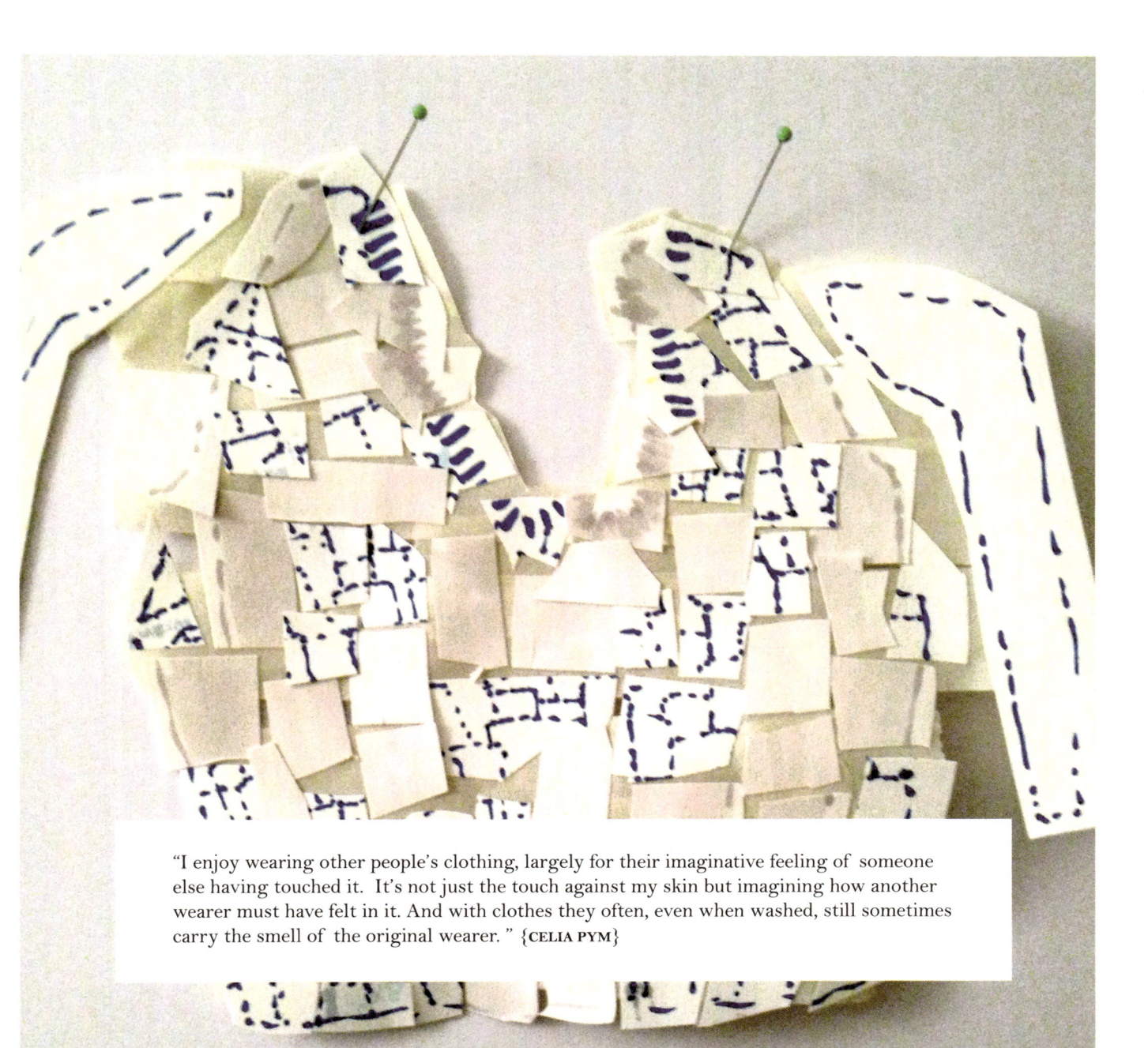

"I enjoy wearing other people's clothing, largely for their imaginative feeling of someone else having touched it. It's not just the touch against my skin but imagining how another wearer must have felt in it. And with clothes they often, even when washed, still sometimes carry the smell of the original wearer." {CELIA PYM}

CELIA PYM {UK}

In the transition from the body to space, between remembrance and expectations, past and present, fragility and transience, I explore visual possibilities. Something occurs, resolves, alters and connects. Mental and physical conditions. It has to do with breathing and rhythm, hands and yarn, slow and close. The leftovers, cast-offs, the lost and incomplete, are all important elements in my installations. I work with the remains of textiles, when something is unravelled it can begin all over again. A well-used knitted garment can encompass everything from daily events to great dramas. It is as though a personal handwriting is embedded in the yarn. If we unravel it, we can still see the wavy traces of the stitches and they aren´t easily washed away. 'Legacies' consists of around 80 spools of yarn created from the same amount of unravelled clothing and hand knitted sweaters. The coils are carriers of time and thoughts, sorrows and joys, hopes and dreams. With drawings and stories on the floor the threads run from the bobbins and are knitted together in a new piece of clothing.

KARI STEIHAUG {NORWAY}

TITLE: LEGACIES
INSTALLATION: variable sizes
MATERIALS: unravelled knitted wool clothes, threads, spools of yarn, knitted sweater
IMAGES: Roar Øhlander

KARI STEIHAUG {NORWAY}

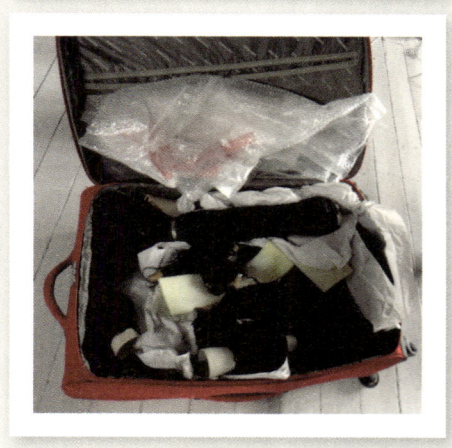

"When I found my unfinished knitting projects again, I remembered the stories embedded in small beginnings and the unfinished garments, all the memories that sat in my body.

I remembered the pleasure and expectation when beginning something new, the thought of how fine it would be. I remembered a love affair who didn't last long enough for him to receive the patterned sweater I was knitting for him, and I remembered all that changed along the way. Memories about things failed and lost.

Some years later this became the starting point of my ongoing project: 'Archive: The Unfinished Ones'." {KARI STEIHAUG}

CURATOR'S NOTES: "One of Norway's foremost textile artists, I have wanted to work with Kari Steihaug since 2006 when I first saw her installation of garments that had been knitted, used, washed, dried, folded, stacked, used, washed and folded again. Layers of time. Horizontal and vertical. And this exhibition has provided the opportunity. If our identity is dependent on our memories: we are what we remember, then when the memories fade away they take our identity with us. The unravelling garment hangs high with its waterfall of threads that are rewinding around the bobbins, returning to an earlier state. The permanent kinks in the threads as they rewind onto the bobbins are the link between the past and present, between the experience and the remembering. This disappearing garment with its implicit traces becomes a metaphor for the vanishing self through loss of memory." {LESLEY MILLAR}

KARI STEIHAUG {NORWAY}

This work is inspired by my previous work, 'MA', which I created during my stay in Manchester and showed in the 'Textural Space' exhibition. In Japan, a look of age on artwork is associated with the passage of time and thought to be an aspect of exquisite taste. As I was exploring how I could express the ten years of time since the work was given birth, I thought about the idea of "look of age". In order to create the look, I am showing it with my current work made from polypropylene. Cubes, from my current work, are floating in the holes of the previous work.

KOJI TAKAKI {JAPAN}

TITLE: MA - INSTALLATION - MATERIALS: polypropylene, cotton cloth

KOJI TAKAKI {JAPAN}

CURATOR'S NOTES: "The work in this exhibition is the materialisation of memory in many ways - firstly it is made up from two separate works, made in different places and different times. The structure is a part of a work Koji Takaki made and exhibited in Manchester in 2001 as a site-specific commission for the Whitworth Art Gallery as part of the exhibition 'Textural Space'. The processes involved in making this work are time based, the material is washed hundreds of times until the fibres begin to break down, the work was then hung outside in the Manchester (rainy) weather for two months and the fibres continued to break down. The cloth, the work, contains both the emotional and the physical memories of the artist and the place. The translucent cubes are part of a much more recent work, made and exhibited in Japan. As installed, the cubes appear to float in and out of the main structure, connecting and moving away Bringing the two works together and showing the result back in the UK is yet another step in a continuously evolving work. It also has a very personal connection for me as I was the curator of 'Textural Space'." {LESLEY MILLAR}

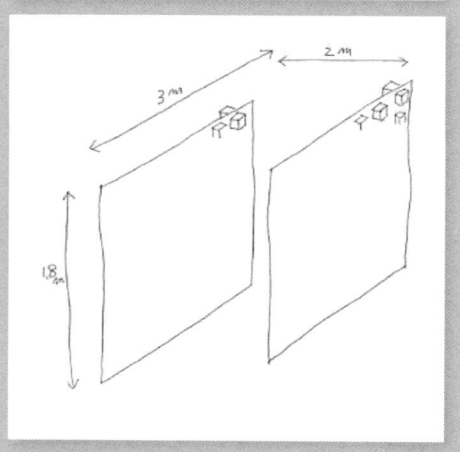

"When I was young, I loved the carp-shaped banners that are displayed on Boys' Day. My first memory of textiles is watching these huge carp swimming in the sky." {KOJI TAKAKI}

KOJI TAKAKI {JAPAN}

INTERVIEW - KATSURA TAKASUKA - 18 FEBRUARY 2013 {TOKYO}

"As I am working, I am touching life past - and I wonder why I am doing this. The material I am using is actually the material of life. I have always been trying to make light, transparent cloth, one that people can wrap around themselves, but now I wanted to make a more concentrated form. One cannot calculate the weight of a life. A cocoon is 0.5 grams and my cube is 2 kilos, which equals 2,000 cocoons - the weight of life, no waste. Even when I am working with waste materials as with the cubes, I am making waste. I realised that spending 2 months of my life to make one piece was my way of expressing my thanks to the material. This project helped me think about life: density and time. Previously, using my fingers I could transform the fibres to make beautiful cloth. With these new works it seems that the cubes are something like a grave, a memorial to life and materials."

KATSURA TAKASUKA {JAPAN}

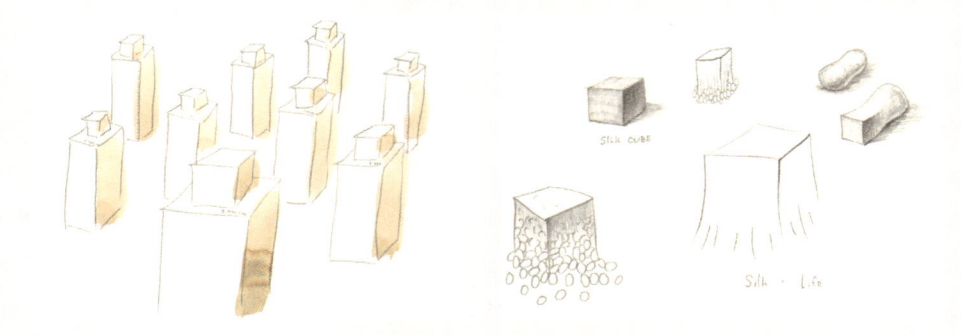

TITLE: SOULS
INSTALLATION: 13 pieces, each 13 × 13 × 13cm
MATERIAL: silk

KATSURA TAKASUKA {JAPAN}

"When I was a child, my mother taught me how to knit. I can remember the joy and amazement at how my hands could transform something as basic as yarn into tangible objects such as gloves or a scarf..." {KATSURA TAKASUKA}

CURATOR'S NOTES: "I was introduced to Katsura Takasuka and his work by the eminent textile designer Reiko Sudo and I was immediately engaged by his passionate commitment to the ideas underlying his work. His sketch books and journals overflowed with drawings, samples, ideas, and his need to alert us to the importance of traditional practice, of nature and the dangers inherent in the loss of contact with both. From his large bag, like a magician, he produced beautifully wrapped shapes, which he carefully revealed as some of his silk cubes.

Each cube weighs 2 kilos and is made from silk cocoons which each weigh 0.5 grammes. The density of the form is intense: an accumulation of weightlessness, which finally achieves its due weight: the passing of life or as he calls it 'The Weight of Life'. As the hair's breadth silk is unwound from the cocoon onto the metal spindle the centre becomes compacted by the natural glue and cannot be used. The thread of that most precious of fibres, silk, pressed, compacted and abandoned until, with so much patience, removed and layered, one infinitesimal layer on another, by Takasuka. His use of these waste silk fibres resonate with ideas of value, memory and time." {LESLEY MILLAR}

KATSURA TAKASUKA {JAPAN}

I use computer programmed sewing machines to make my work. I can programme stitches with pinpoint accuracy, fill areas with decorative satin stitch and build images with precision: I can make in a way that I could not have imagined when I graduated 25 years ago. Technology is allowing me to create and adapt imagery in a way that I never expected. It feels like the possibilities are endless.

KARINA THOMPSON {UK}

This piece seeks to visualise a physical response to my first experience of visiting the Spinning Room at Salts Mill. The room is 168m long; a tenth of a mile. The mill, when in full production was reported to have made 18 miles of cloth a day; 1½ miles an hour, 15 lengths of the Spinning Room. For me the first time I entered the room I had an overwhelming desire to run the length of it, and probably would have done if not in the company of strangers.

But I did come back and ran 1½ miles representing an hour's cloth production. I wore a monitor to record my heartbeats and printed my running footprints by using the dust of the mill onto strips of paper. This data is used in this piece. The red ECG line shows how my heart rate went from 68bpm to 181bpm. The embroidered footprints are based on those prints taken on the run. The ultrasound triangles show how the chambers of my heart open and close on a heartbeat.

I hope the embroidery accurately represents my running gait overstitched with heart data showing the electrical and physical activity of my heart as I travelled across the room. I want to make permanent the memory of the transient movements of both my heart and feet whilst I ran in the space.

TITLE: 1 HOUR'S PRODUCTION = 1 ½ MILES = 15 LENGTHS
INSTALLATION: 100 x 0.5 metres
MATERIALS: woollen cloth, non woven stabiliser, rayon, polyester, lurex and metallic thread

KARINA THOMPSON {UK}

"My mother studied embroidery at Goldsmiths under Constance Howard in the 1950's before going into teaching. My earliest memory of a picture in a frame was one of her embroideries above the kitchen table.

I remember being very young, perhaps five or six, and being put in an empty classroom whilst my mother was next door in a meeting. The school was empty. She put me down with a huge pile of assorted materials with the suggestion that I should make a 'fabric collage'. She started me out with simple geometric shapes suggesting a cityscape. The background was dark turquoise. I cut similar shapes and stuck them down with Copydex. I really enjoyed it and was very proud of my work although that day I learnt that Copydex wasn't the best adhesive for sheer fabric 'clouds'.

When I was little I grew up surrounded by my mother's embroideries on the walls. I thought all Mums did that stuff. I thought that was what you did when you grew up; you made fabric pictures."
{KARINA THOMPSON}

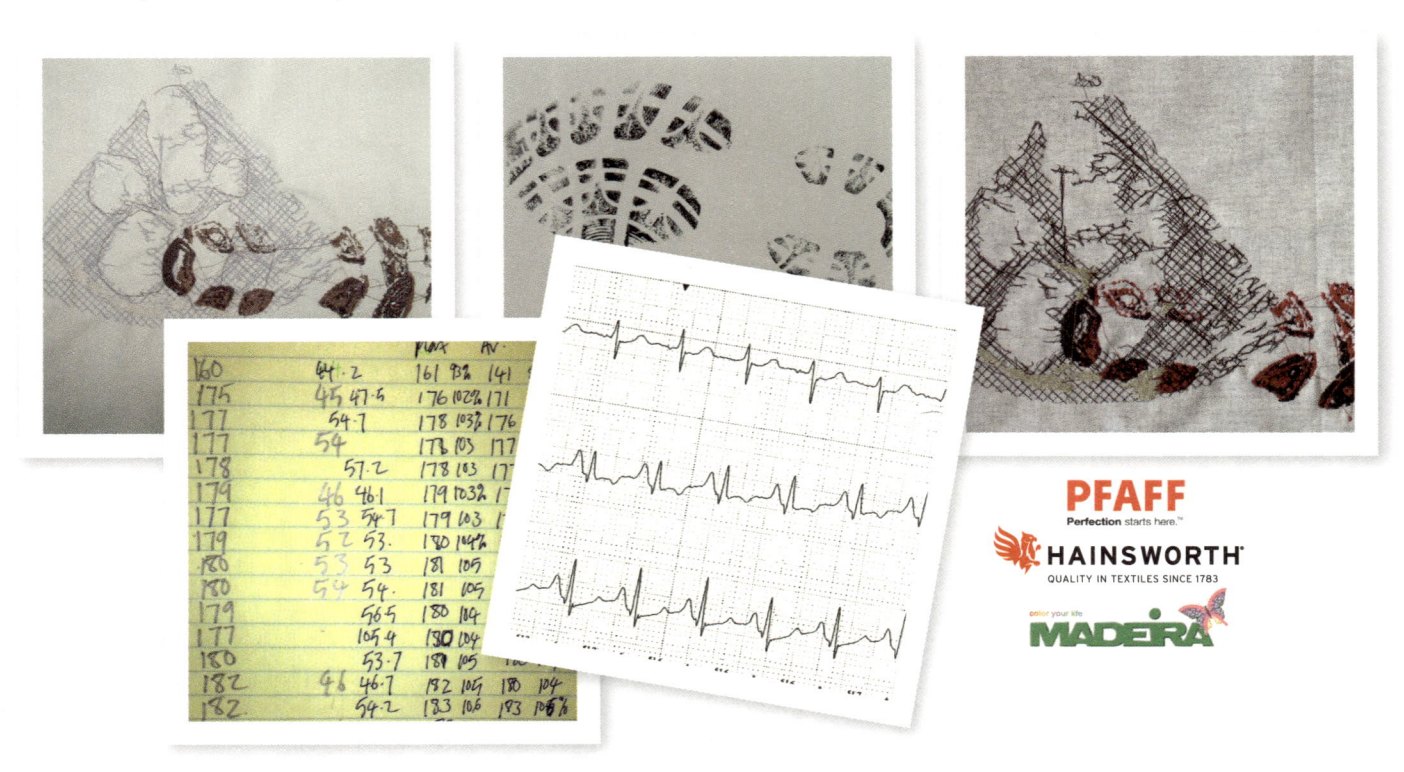

SPONSORS: Pfaff (sewing machines), Hainsworth (woollen cloth), Madeira (rayon thread), Arnold Laver (wood) Thanks to Nicky Smith and the Cardiology Department at the Queen Elizabeth Hospital, Birmingham for their help

IMAGE OPPOSITE: Hannah Coaten

CURATOR'S NOTES: "Karina Thompson's work is completely about her body being in this space, moving through the space, connecting with the floor, feeling the impact of the floor through her body as she runs up and down, monitoring the corporeal effects, as she physically becomes the space. In her actions she is echoing the daily journeys of the workers as they walked up and down the room. What we see are the translated traces of the experience: her footprints made from the dust on the floor, her heart rate as recorded on the ECG, the changes in the muscles of the heart - all the physical responses to her interaction with the room re-created through stitch. It is a huge piece, as befits the space, and it is covered with the most intimate of images, taken from the hidden and interior responses of her body and the ephemeral traces of her presence." {LESLEY MILLAR}

KARINA THOMPSON {UK}

Rice is very valuable, grown over a long period of time and with very much serious effort . I cannot afford to lose a single grain. It satisfies the hungry people, and workers. Not only is it food, but a thing of value as well , in the past has been used as a substitute for money and also in the architectural environment as excellent natural adhesive. However, now in Japan, it is sometimes discarded as leftovers, and its value has been lost. Rice leftovers, which have lost their function, are discarded as trash, but every grain when it is dried, is translucent once exposed to light, each grain is like a beautiful shining jewel and I think it more precious than jewels.

YORIKO YONEYAMA {JAPAN}

The outside appearance of Salts Mill, a World Heritage Site, is not anything special at first glance, it looks like a harmonious building of 100 years before. Here, it is intended to convey to the future, what you see is not special, but the town was made in order to safeguard the health of the workers whose environment was poor during the industrial revolution, and that this fact is why this is a cultural heritage.

I think it is significant that by exhibiting rice, which is valuable and precious for the Japanese, at this location, which was made under the concept that workers as "human beings" are valuable, it makes sense to think about what we should leave to the future.

"When I was young, my mother made clothes using not only needles, thread and scissors but also glue, a hammer, even a chisel. As I sat by her side watching, I would take small scraps of fabric and thread to play with, or to make clothes for my dolls." {YORIKO YONEYAMA}

TITLE: RICE DREAMS 2013 SALTS MILL
INSTALLATION: 10 x 5 metres
MATERIALS: rice, silk threads, mirrors

YORIKO YONEYAMA {JAPAN}

CURATOR'S NOTES: "The painstaking concentration and commitment required to create her 'Rice Dreams' is almost beyond comprehension. Every cooked grain of rice is placed by hand onto the fine silk threads, the natural starch of the rice means that the grain will adhere to the thread as it dries. How many grains of rice in an installation? Impossible to count. In this installation Yoneyama is reflecting on the relationship between the central role and value that both rice and wool have had within societies and that they are now overlooked and not regarded. By creating an art work from the rice she is giving it a new value. The effect is overwhelming in its delicate, beauty - the whole seeming like rainfall onto the 'water' mirrors below. The mirrors themselves are chosen because they hold the memory of all who have looked into them." {LESLEY MILLAR}

YORIKO YONEYAMA {JAPAN}

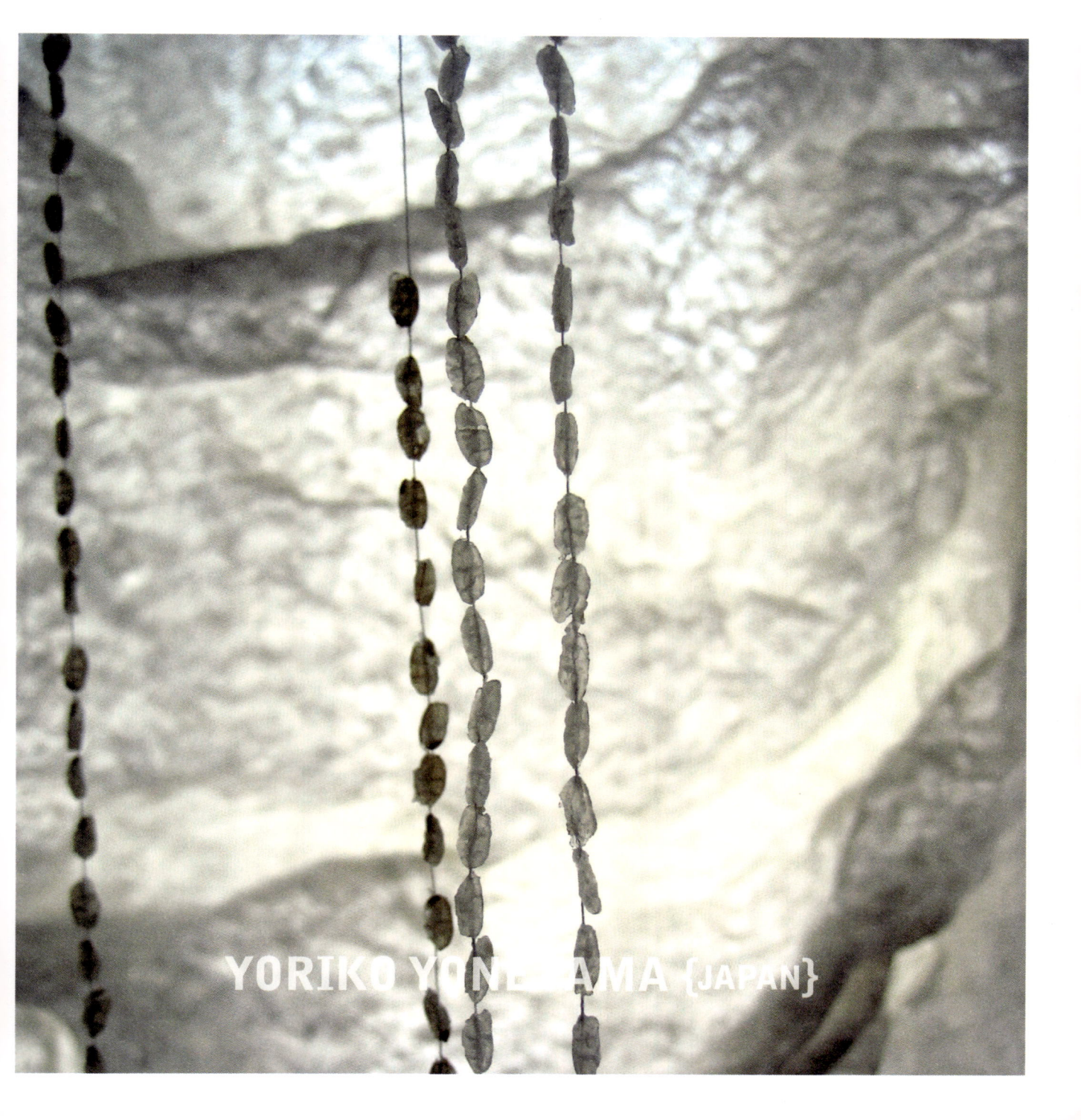

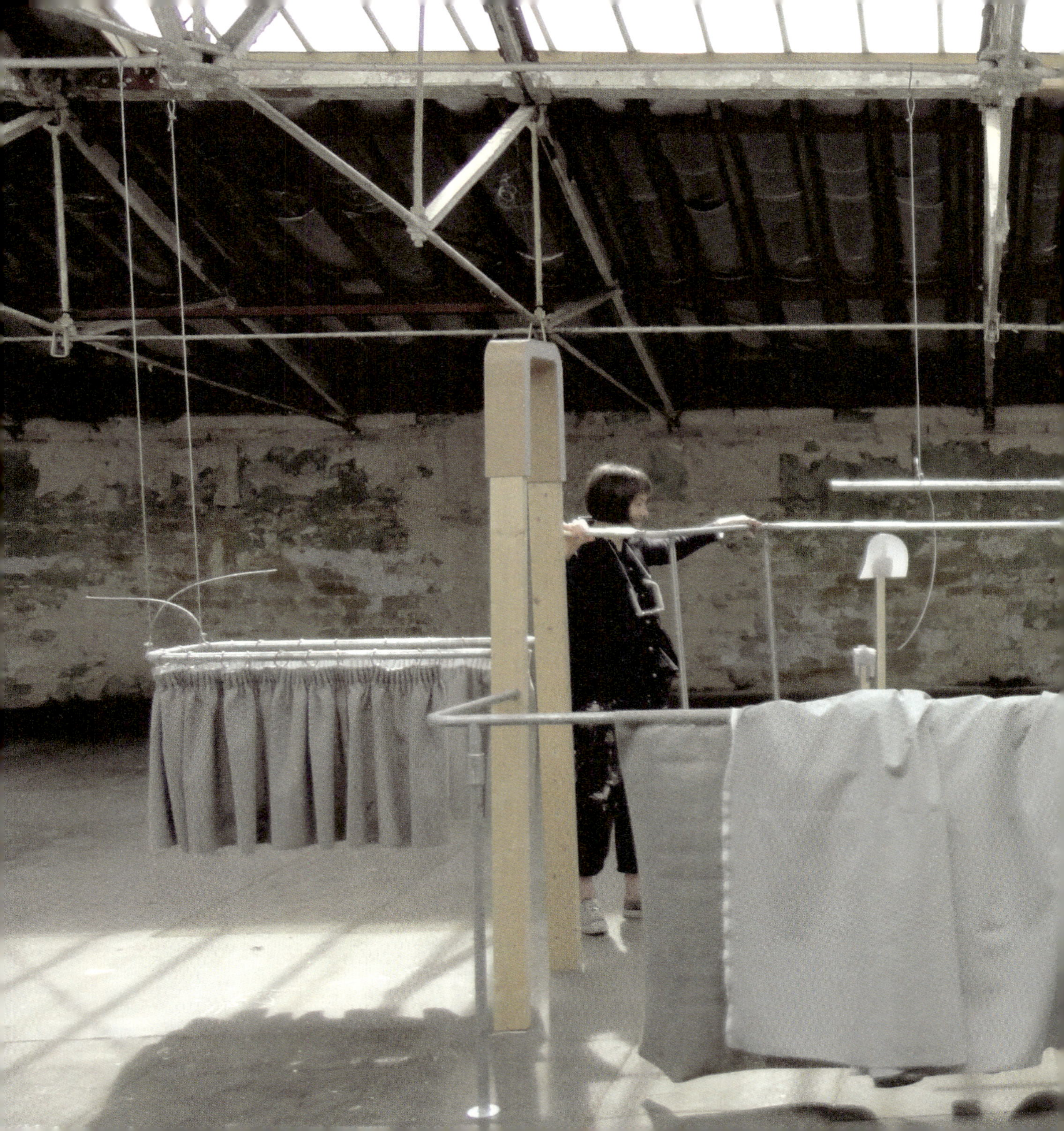

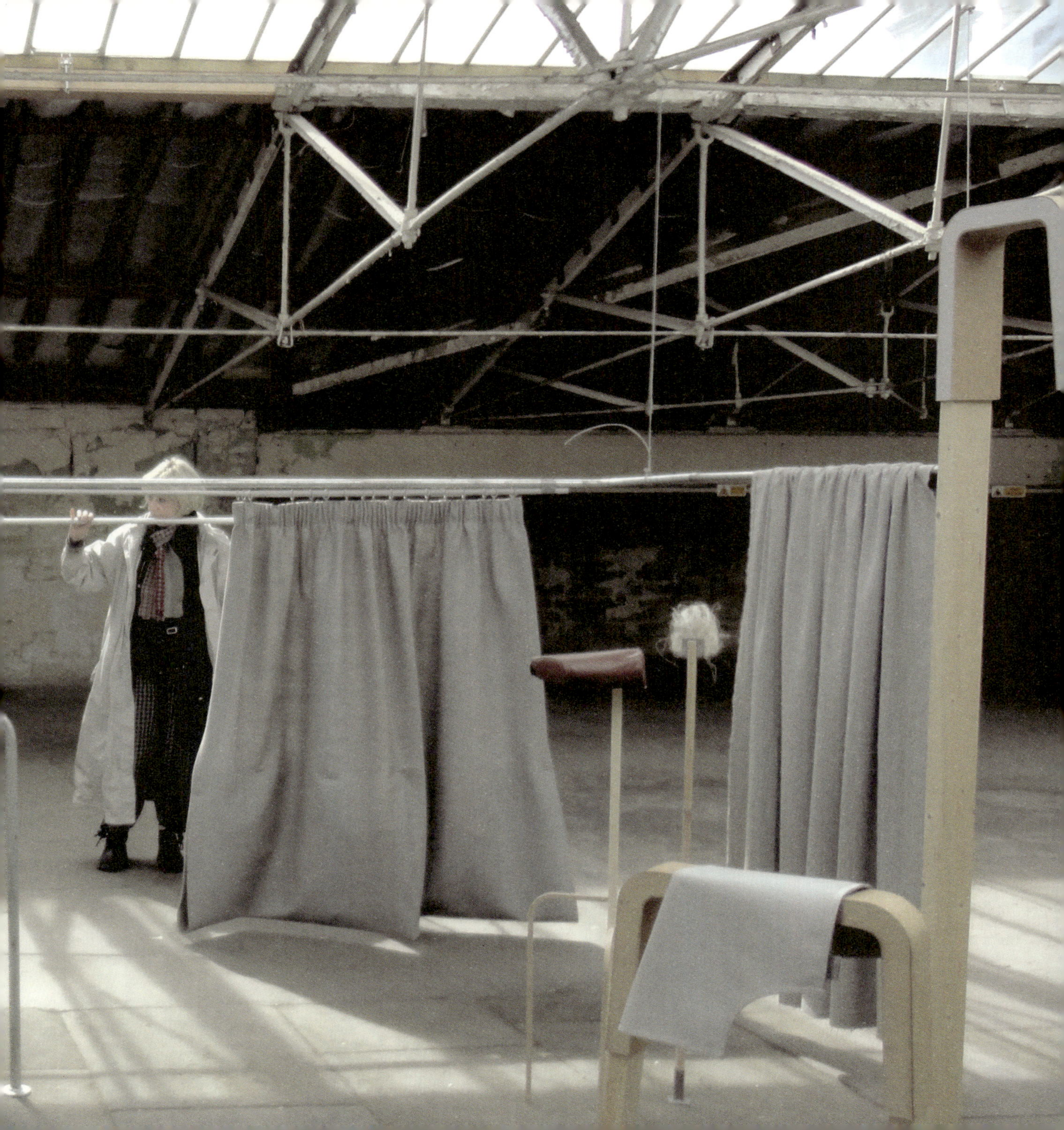

MACHIKO AGANO {JAPAN}

Recent exhibitions & projects

2012	Contemporary Japanese Fiber Art Exhibition, San Francisco Craft and Folklore Art Museum, San Francisco USA
2011	7th International Textile Triennial, Tournai, Belgium
	Contemporary Japanese Fiber Art Exhibition, Tama Art Gallery, Tokyo Japan, Japan Society, NY USA
	'a prefix': Hyogo Prefectural Museum, Japan; Western Australian Museum, Perth, Australia
	'Bite-Size: Miniature Textiles from Japan and The UK': Daiwa Foundation, London UK and GalleryGallery, Kyoto; NUA Japan

Selected commissions & awards

2007	Kyoto Art and Culture Prize
1992	2nd Contemporary Crafts Exhibition by Selected Artists Excellence Award

JEANETTE APPLETON {UK}

Recent exhibitions & projects

2012	'Interventions', Platt Hall
	'Radical Thread', The 62 Group of Textile Artists, 50th Anniversary Exhibition, The Holden Gallery, Manchester
2011	'Bite-Size: Miniature Textiles from Japan and The UK', Daiwa Foundation, London UK and Gallery Gallery, Kyoto
2010	'Travelling Lines' Solo show, Loft Gallery, Farfield Mill, Sedbergh, Cumbria
	'Bending More Lines' touring to Rijswijk Gallery, Holland and Collins Gallery, Glasgow, Scotland with The 62 Group of Textile Artists
2009-7	'Sow:Sew' solo shows touring to: Farfield Mill, Sedbergh; Myles Meehan Gallery, Darlington Arts Centre; John Innes Centre, Norwich; Bankfield Museum, Halifax; The Knitting and Stitching shows in four venues Gallery Oldham and Quay Arts, Isle of Wight

Selected commissions & awards

2007	ACE National Touring program award for solo show 'Sow:Sew'
2003	ACE funding for the 'Through The Surface' project on the International Artist Fellowship Programme and by the University of Huddersfield

MASAE BAMBA {JAPAN}

Recent exhibitions & projects

2012	Gion Matsuri exhibition, Kyoto, Japan
2011	'Re:a prefix', Kobe, Japan
	18th Seiryuten-Some exhibition, Kyoto, Japan
	'Bite-Size: Miniature Textiles from Japan and The UK', Daiwa Foundation, London UK and Gallery Gallery, Kyoto
	Solo exhibition, Gallery Nekogameya, Osaka, Japan

CAROLINE BARTLETT {UK}

Recent exhibitions & projects

2012	'Radical Thread', The 62 Group of Textile Artists, 50th Anniversary Exhibition, The Holden Gallery, Manchester
2011	'Stimulus', Browngrotta Arts, Connecticut, USA
2010	'Focus' and 'Black and White': Contemporary Applied Arts, London; Circus, London
2009-10	'Bending the Line': Hub National Centre for Craft and Design, Sleaford, UK; Rijswijk, The Hague, Nederlands; Collins Gallery, Glasgow
2007	'Collect', Victoria and Albert Museum, London

Selected commissions & awards

2011	Black Swan Arts Award; First Prize
2003	Commissioned by the Whitworth Art Gallery, Manchester, UK

HILARY BOWER {UK}

Recent exhibitions & projects

2012	'Radical Thread', The 62 Group of Textile Artists, 50th Anniversary Exhibition, The Holden Gallery, Manchester
2011	'The Cut', Halesworth Arts Festival
2010	'Bending the Line', The 62 Group of Textile Artists, The HUB, Sleaford, Lincolnshire
2009	Stroud International Textile Festival
2008	Walford Mill Crafts, Dorset

Selected commissions & awards

Awarded a Research and Development Grant by the Arts Council England Yorkshire in 2006 for work developed and made for a major solo exhibition in 2006/2007

MAXINE BRISTOW {UK}

Recent exhibitions & projects

2013	'Staging (and restaging) the specific unspecificity of textile (and other things)', Site specific interventions, Whitworth Art Gallery
2012	'Transformations' (group exhibition), Smiths Row, Bury St Edmunds
2011	'Z Depth Buffer' (joint exhibition with Sally Morfill), 5 Years Gallery, London
	'Bite-Size: Miniature Textiles from Japan and The UK': Daiwa Foundation, London UK and GalleryGallery, Kyoto; NUA Japan
2008	'Cloth and Culture Now' (group exhibition), Sainsbury Centre for Visual Arts, Norwich

Selected commissions & awards

2008	Nominated, Northern Arts Prize
2002	Shortlisted, Jerwood Applied Arts Prize: Textiles. Crafts Council, London

REECE CLEMENTS {UK}

Recent exhibitions & projects

2012	Cardiff School of Art and Design Degree Show, Cardiff
2012	'Seven/Saith', Oriel Canfas, Cardiff
2009	Bradford College Course Show, Bradford

Selected commissions & awards

2012	The Lavinia Bletchley Memorial Award

YASUKO FUJINO {JAPAN}

Recent exhibitions & projects

2012	International Tapestry Exhibition, Kyoto Art Center
2010	Solo exhibition, Gallert Keifu
2008	Tapestry 2008, Australian National University, School of Art Gallery
2007	Fiberart International, Pittsburgh, USA
2005	5th Triennial International Tapestry and Textile Art Exhibition, Tournai, Belgium

Selected commissions & awards

1999	The Museum of Kyoto
1994	The Museum of Kyoto
1992	Yodogawa Christian Hospital, Osaka

CAREN GARFEN {UK}

Recent exhibitions & projects

2013	Internationale d'Art Miniature, Quebec, Canada
	Featured Artist, The Beetroot Tree, Derbyshire
	'Small Talk', The 62 Group of Textile Artists, Constance Howard Research Centre, Goldsmiths College, London
	Nadelwerke (Needle Works), Galerie Handwerk, Munich, Germany
2012	Royal Academy of Arts Summer Exhibition, London

Selected commissions & awards

2012	Work of the Week, Royal Academy of Arts Summer Exhibition
2010	V&A Museum commission for 'Quilts 1700-2010 Hidden Histories Untold Stories'

RACHEL GRAY {UK}

Recent exhibitions & projects

2012	MAde, James Hockey Gallery, UCA Farnham
2011	MAde, James Hockey Gallery, UCA Farnham

ANNIE HARRISON {UK}

Recent exhibitions & projects

2013	The Heinrich Event, Rogue Project Space, Manchester
2012	Rogue Open Studios, Manchester
2011	'Manchester Time Piece', with Tern Collective
	'Uncovered,' site specific installation, Farfield Mill, Sedbergh
2010	'Untitled', site specific installation, Platt Hall Costume Gallery

Selected commissions & awards

2008	Manchester School of Art Travel Award
2009	'Lost rivers', textile commission for Headquarters of Baker Tilly, Manchester

DIANA HARRISON {UK}

Recent exhibitions & projects

2011	'Bite-Size: Miniature Textiles from Japan and The UK', Daiwa Foundation, London UK and GalleryGallery, Kyoto
	'Lost in Lace', Birmingham City Art Gallery UK
2010	Demain, Centre de Recerche et de Design en Impression Textile, Montreal, Quebec
	35/35 Contemporary European Art Quilts, Musee D'art d'Histoire, Neuchatel, Switzerland
	'Quilts 1700-2010 Hidden Histories, Untold Stories', Victoria and Albert Museum London

Selected commissions & awards

2005	Winner of 'Quilt 2005', The Quilt Festival, NEC Birmingham
2003	Silver Award for Contemporary Entry, 7th Quilt Nihon Exhibition, Tokyo

KATHARINA HINSBERG {GERMANY}

Recent exhibitions & projects

2013	'linie, line, linea', Centro de Arte Contemporáneo de Quito, Quito, Ecuador
2012	'Feldern (Die Teile und das Ganze)', Kunstverein Ulm, Germany (Solo exhibition)
	'Rasterfahndung. Das Raster in der Kunst nach 1945', Kunstmuseum Stuttgart, Germany
	'Le bruit du dessin', Centre d'art contemporain d'Annemasse, Annemasse, France
2011	'Lost in Lace', Birmingham Museum and Art Gallery, UK

Selected commissions & awards

2011	Art in Public Space, University of Saarbrucken, Germany
2010	Award for a permanent Wall Work at the Ministery of Agriculture, Berlin, Germany

PHILIPPA LAWRENCE {UK}

Recent exhibitions & projects

2011	'Bite-Size: Miniature Textiles from Japan and The UK': Daiwa Foundation, London UK and GalleryGallery, Kyoto; NUA Japan
2012	'Sub-Woofer', Spike Island, Bristol
2011	'Nature Unframed', Morton Arboretum, Chicago, USA
2010	Celebrating Paper, Royal West Academy, Bristol
2009	'Tell it to the Trees', Meadow Arts at Croft Castle, Leominster

Selected commissions & awards

2013	'Darning the Land: Sewn', Waddesdon Manor, Aylesbury
2011	'Barcode FB814', Mortimer Forest, ACE Rural Commissioning Programme

PETA JACOBS {UK}

Recent exhibitions & projects

2012	MAde, James Hockey Gallery, UCA Farnham
	'Hidden Spaces, Hidden Places', Mall Galleries, London
	Nagoya University of the Arts, Japan
2011	MAde, James Hockey Gallery, UCA Farnham
2010	New Designers, Business Design Centre, Islington, London

Selected commissions & awards

2010	31st Takifuji International Art Award (Japan).

HANNAH LEIGHTON-BOYCE {UK}

Recent exhibitions & projects

2013	'Handmade futures' Blank Media Collective, Manchester
	The Frost Art Museum Drawing Project, The Frost Art Museum, Miami
	Through Neo, gallery22, Bolton
	'RULE OF 3' Residency, Islington Mill, Salford
2012	MA Show, The Holden Gallery, Manchester School of Art

Selected commissions & awards

2012	Textile Society Postgraduate Bursary Winner
2010	Arts and Humanities Research Council Postgraduate Funding

YORIKO MURAYAMA {JAPAN}

Recent exhibitions & projects

2011	'Re: a prefix' Exhibition, WA Museum Perth Australia, Hyogo Prefectural Museum of Art, Japan
2011	Miniartextile, installation part, Como Italy
2011	Solo exhibition, GalleryGallery, Kyoto, Japan
2010	13th International Triennial of Tapestry, Lodz Poland
2006	Ex. Changing Tradition Exhibition, Perth Australia, Kyoto Art Centre, Japan

Selected commissions & awards

2003	Collection award Art Gallery of Szombathely, Hungary
1996	Collection award Art Gallery of Szombathely, Hungary
1980	New Face Textile Exhibition (Grand Prize Award). Kyoto Japan

CELIA PYM {UK}

Recent exhibitions & projects

2013	'No excuse for what I do in private', curated by Matt Rich, Delicious Spectacle, Washington DC, USA
2012	Art and Anatomy, Gordon Museum of Pathology, KCL, London
2011	'Bite-Size: Miniature Textiles from Japan and The UK': Daiwa Foundation, London UK and GalleryGallery, Kyoto; NUA Japan
	'Missed/Missing', Textile Arts Center, Brooklyn, New York, USA
2010	'outside-in', Aichi Trienniale, Nagoya, Japan

Selected commissions & awards

2010	Selected for Curatorial Competition, Aichi Trienniale, Nagoya, Japan
2001	Gardner Fellowship, one-year travel fellowship, Harvard University

KARI STEIHAUG {NORWAY}

Recent exhibitions & projects

2013	'A stitch in time', Haugar Art Museum, Tønsberg
2012	'No / NOoSPHERE Neverending Story', New York
2012	The Art of Collecting, Tallin
2012	The Spring Exhibition, 'Archive: The Unfinished Ones' Arthall Charlottenborg, Copenhagen
2012	After The Market Gallery, Naas, Gothenburg

Selected commissions & awards

2012	Audience award, The Spring Exhibition, Arthall Charlottenborg, for 'Archive: The Unfinished Ones,
2011	Fine Art award, The Annual Exhibition, for the installation 'After the Market'

KOJI TAKAKI {JAPAN}

Recent exhibitions & projects

2011	GalleryGallery, Kyoto, Japan
2011	'Bite-Size: Miniature Textiles from Japan and The UK', Daiwa Foundation, London UK and GalleryGallery, Kyoto
	WA-Hyogo Sister State Exchange Textile, Fibre Art exhibition, 'Re: a prefix'
2009	Gallery 16, Kyoto, Japan
2007	The 12th International Triennial of Tapestry, Lodz, Poland/Central Museum of Textile
	'Japanese Suppleness' Frederiksvaerk and Fredericia Denmark

KATSURA TAKASUKA {JAPAN}

Recent exhibitions & projects

2012	Natural materials for textile IV in Tohkamachi, Cross 10
2011	'I love silk', The Museum of Modern Art, Gunma
2011	The Japan Contemporary Fiber Art Exhibition, Tama Art University Museum
2009	Solo Exhibition, Galerie Lauran
2008	TSUTSUMU Exhibition, Tokyo - Sweden Abroad

Selected commissions & awards

2009	Mitsubishi Chemical Junior Designer Award, 'Saibaiman'
2009	MOLESKINE 'My Detour Tokyo' Outstanding Performance Award

KARINA THOMPSON {UK}

Recent exhibitions & projects

2013	Quilt Art, Tsaritsyno Museum of Applied Art, Moscow
2012	5th European Quilt Triennale, Textilsammlung Max Berk, Kurpfälzisches Museum, Heidelberg, Germany
	'Made in the Middle', Mac, Birmingham and the Hub, Sleaford
2010	ITAB: International TECHstyle Art Biennial, San Jose, California
	EXNA IV, Museum of Art and History of Neuchâtel, Switzerland

Selected commissions & awards

2010	'Making Moves' residency at Soho House, Birmingham
2009	Series of embroidered wall pieces, Centre for Clinical Haematology, University Hospital, Birmingham

YORIKO YONEYAMA {JAPAN}

Recent exhibitions & projects

2011	Conservatorio dell'Aquila Concert Hall, Italy
2011	"Position 2011" Nagoya City Art Museum, Aichi
2010	"Rice Dreams" Aichi Triennale, Joint Activities with Nanatsudera Kyodo Studio Aichi
2010	Ikebana International, The Wilanow Palace Museum, Poland
2009	'Kome No Yume' penelope paris petillante, Aichi

Selected commissions & awards

1985	PARCO Award, Japan Objects Award, Second Prize, Japan

ACKNOWLEDGEMENTS

A huge thank you to Maggie Silver for her generosity and unstinting support through all the trials and tribulations that we have encountered and for giving us the opportunity to hold this exhibition in the wonderfully inspiring Salts Mill. Special thanks to Zoë Silver for her introduction in the catalogue to the background to Salts Mill today and for her support from the very beginning, to Linda Wilkinson for all her help and patiently answering all our questions, to Sue Roe, Bookshop Manager and her team who have done so much to facilitate the exhibition, to Steve Mason for his patience and expertise, and to all the staff at Salts Mill.

Thank you to Dr Simon Ofield-Kerr, Vice-Chancellor, the University for the Creative Arts, for his introduction in the catalogue outlining the importance of the project within the current education climate. Thank you to all our funders and sponsors - the exhibition could not have happened without their support; and also to Maggie Pedley, Museums and Galleries Manager at Bradford Museums & Galleries and all her staff who have gone out of their way to help artists in their archival searches.

Thank you, as ever, to Gerry Diebel and his team at Direct Design for the advice and input which has resulted in yet another beautiful catalogue and very special thanks to Beverly Ayling-Smith for her hard work on all aspects of the project. Grateful thanks to all those who have offered technical help, particularly Richard Jones, Tipu Miah, Peter Walshaw from UCA and Sebastian White, and all the volunteers drawn from current and recent graduates from UCA, Manchester Metropolitan University, and the University of Huddersfield. And most especially thank you to all the artists for their remarkable responses to Salts Mill.

THE CLOTH & MEMORY TEAM

"I remember when I was a child licking bits of red ribbon for quite a long time. It gave you a very good lipstick – it came over the edges of the lips a bit, but it was good."

THE CLOTH & MEMORY TEAM

LESLEY MILLAR: Lesley Millar has worked as an exhibition organiser and curator specialising in textiles since 1987 and has been project director for 7 major international touring exhibitions: 'Revelation' (1996-98), 'Textural Space' (2001), 'Through the Surface' (2003-05), '21:21 – the textile vision of Reiko Sudo and NUNO' (2005-7), 'Cloth & Culture NOW' (2008), 'Cultex: textiles as a cross-cultural language' (2009-11), and 'Lost in Lace' (2011-12.). She is currently leading on an EU funded collaboration between the UK, Denmark, Greece and Italy: 'Transparent Boundaries' (2012-13).

She writes regularly about contemporary textile practice, particularly that in Britain and Japan. In 2005 she was appointed Director of the Anglo Japanese Textile Research Centre at the University for the Creative Arts. In 2008 she received the Japan Society Award for her contribution to Anglo-Japanese relationships. In 2007 was appointed Professor of Textile Culture at UCA and in 2011 was awarded an MBE for her contribution to Higher Education.

JUNE HILL: June Hill is a Bradford based freelance writer/curator. Her work focuses on the relationship between, and contextualisation of, historic textiles and contemporary practice. She is also interested in the role and place of process. June has been publishing ongoing research into UK textile collections in Embroidery since January 2006; is the author/editor of several artist monographs and a contributor to The Textile Reader (Berg 2012) and Outside: Activating Cloth to Enhance the Way We Live (CSP 2014). Recent projects include: 'Crafting Hope: The Sleeping Bag Project' with Claire Barber, University of Huddersfield and 'Forever Changes: Michael Brennand-Wood' (Ruthin Craft Centre and tour). She is currently curating a further exhibition for Ruthin on Goldsmiths Textile Department 1975-88.

JENNIFER HALLAM: Jennifer Hallam has curated numerous fine art and craft exhibitions, often in partnership with artists and museums across the United Kingdom, Europe and America. Moving into the arts funding system, she worked with artists, organisations and other agencies to create new opportunities for the production and presentation of work. The latter included capital projects resulting in new studio spaces such as Persistence Works, Sheffield and The Art House, Wakefield, and new venues such as The Gallery at Ryedale Folk Museum and The Hepworth Wakefield. She has worked on a freelance basis since 2010, primarily with museums and galleries across Yorkshire.

KEIKO KAWASHIMA: Keiko Kawashima is the Director of the Kyoto International Contemporary Art Centre at Gallery Gallery in Kyoto, Japan. She has worked extensively in Australia and in Eastern Europe and has worked with Lesley Millar as Co-ordinator in Japan since 1998.